How to Answer Rude People without Getting Fired

Learn Tactful Responses for Tricky Situations

Gene Pan

DISCLAIMER

While every precaution has been taken in the preparation of this book, the publisher assumes no responsibility for errors or omissions, or for damages resulting from the use of the information contained herein.

How to Answer Rude People without Getting Fired: Learn Tactful Responses for Tricky Situations

First edition.

TABLE OF CONTENTS

PART I

Understanding Rude Behavior

INTRODUCTION

DEFINING RUDENESS

TYPES OF RUDENESS (DIRECT, INDIRECT, PASSIVE-AGGRESSIVE)

Rudeness is an unfortunate reality in both personal and professional environments. Its manifestations can vary widely, but they all have one thing in common: they make interactions uncomfortable, challenging, and often emotionally charged. Understanding the types of rudeness is a crucial first step in responding to them effectively. While rudeness can be direct and explicit, it can also be subtle, cloaked in passive-aggressive behavior, or delivered in an indirect, veiled manner. These different forms of rudeness affect our responses to them, making it essential to recognize the signs and learn how to navigate tricky situations tactfully.

Direct rudeness is the most straightforward and obvious type. It often involves clear, unambiguous insults or derogatory comments that are intended to hurt, belittle, or provoke the target. People engaging in direct rudeness are usually open about their intentions. This might involve someone speaking to you with a harsh tone, using offensive language, making blunt criticisms, or expressing personal attacks. Direct rudeness can occur in public or private settings and is typically easier to identify because the intent to insult or demean is clearly visible.

An example of direct rudeness in a workplace might be a colleague openly criticizing your work in front of others, saying something like, "I don't know how you still have a job here with the mistakes you keep making." Such a statement is not only humiliating but also creates tension and negativity. Direct rudeness can also be seen in dismissive comments, where someone rudely interrupts you, cuts off your explanations, or completely disregards your opinion, like saying, "I don't have time for your ideas, they're always off the mark." These comments are meant to undermine your confidence and can significantly impact your self-esteem and emotional well-being.

Because of its overt nature, direct rudeness can be difficult to ignore, and often, the natural response is to retaliate or defend oneself immediately. However, reacting emotionally or defensively can escalate the situation, potentially leading to conflict or professional repercussions. This is especially true in a work setting, where responses to direct rudeness must be measured and thoughtful. The best approach is often to remain calm and composed, addressing the comment in a neutral tone or even disengaging from the situation if necessary. By staying calm, you maintain control and demonstrate professionalism, even in the face of hostility.

Indirect rudeness, on the other hand, is less overt but no less damaging. It often involves behavior or comments that are disrespectful or hurtful but delivered in a more subtle, roundabout way. Indirect rudeness can be harder to identify because the person being rude may not make their intention clear. It often manifests through actions like ignoring someone's presence, making subtle digs, or failing to acknowledge someone's contribution or effort. This type of behavior leaves the recipient wondering if the slight was intentional or simply accidental, making it more difficult to address.

For instance, imagine you're part of a team working on a project, and during a meeting, one of your colleagues consistently fails to acknowledge your suggestions or contributions. While they may not openly insult you, their dismissive behavior sends a message that your input is not valued. In another case, indirect rudeness might involve someone giving you the cold shoulder, refusing to engage in conversation with you, or making sarcastic remarks that seem innocent on the surface but have an underlying negative tone. This form of rudeness can be particularly frustrating because it creates an ambiguous situation, where it's difficult to discern whether the behavior is intentional or unintentional.

Indirect rudeness can also appear in passive actions, such as arriving late to meetings repeatedly without offering an apology, sending terse or unhelpful emails, or intentionally excluding someone from social or professional gatherings. These actions, while not directly hostile, convey a clear lack of respect or consideration for the other person. Addressing indirect rudeness requires a different approach than dealing with direct rudeness. Instead of confronting the person with accusations, it's often more productive to calmly ask for clarification about their behavior or comment. This opens the door to a constructive conversation and can help resolve misunderstandings while maintaining a professional tone.

The third, and perhaps the most insidious form of rudeness, is passive-aggressive behavior. Passive-aggressiveness is a way of expressing hostility or discontent indirectly, often through behaviors that seem polite or harmless on the surface but carry an undercurrent of resentment or frustration. Passive-aggressive individuals may avoid direct confrontation, but their behavior is no less harmful, as it can create confusion, mistrust, and a toxic work environment. Unlike direct rudeness, passive-aggressiveness often leaves the recipient feeling unsure about how to respond because the message is mixed – the words or actions appear neutral or even kind, but the intent behind them is negative.

A common form of passive-aggressiveness is sarcasm, where someone makes a statement that seems positive or neutral but is actually intended as a veiled criticism. For example, a coworker might say, "Wow, you really outdid yourself on that presentation," but their tone and body language suggest that they're actually mocking your effort. Other examples of passive-aggressive behavior include giving someone the silent treatment, deliberately procrastinating on tasks to inconvenience others, or giving backhanded compliments. For instance, someone might say, "It's amazing you were able to get that report done on time, considering how busy you always seem," which seems like a compliment but carries an underlying jab at your time management skills.

Another hallmark of passive-aggressive behavior is the refusal to communicate openly. Rather than expressing dissatisfaction or frustration directly, the person may act out in subtle ways that leave others guessing about their true feelings. This could involve agreeing to a request but intentionally doing a poor job or complying with the bare minimum effort, with the intention of frustrating the person who made the request. Passive-aggressiveness can also show up in the form of exaggerated politeness, where someone responds to a disagreement or criticism with overly formal, insincere phrases like "Thank you for your input, I'll take it into consideration," without any intention of actually addressing the issue.

Dealing with passive-aggressive behavior is particularly tricky because the person exhibiting it often denies any ill intent, making it difficult to address the underlying issue. Confronting someone about their passive-aggressive behavior can lead to defensiveness or even further passive-aggressiveness, as the person may insist that their behavior was not meant to be harmful. As a result, it's important to approach passive-aggressiveness with patience and understanding. One strategy is to ask open-ended questions that invite the person to express their true feelings in a non-confrontational manner. For example, you might say, "I noticed that you've been quiet about this project lately. Is there something you'd like to discuss?" This can help create an opportunity for the person to express their concerns openly, rather than continuing to engage in passive-aggressive behavior.

It's also helpful to set clear boundaries and expectations when dealing with passive-aggressive individuals. By being upfront about what is and isn't acceptable behavior, you can discourage future instances of passive-aggressiveness. In some cases, it may also be necessary to involve a third party, such as a supervisor or HR representative, to mediate the situation and ensure that the behavior is addressed in a constructive manner.

Understanding the different types of rudeness—whether direct, indirect, or passive-aggressive—empowers you to respond appropriately in each situation. While it may be tempting to react emotionally or defensively, especially when faced with direct insults or passive-aggressive comments, maintaining a calm, composed demeanor allows you to navigate these difficult interactions with grace and professionalism. By recognizing the signs of different types of rudeness and learning how to address them effectively, you can diffuse tension, protect your emotional well-being, and foster a more respectful, positive environment in both your personal and professional life.

The key to handling rudeness lies not only in understanding the different forms it can take but also in developing the emotional intelligence to manage your own responses. Whether faced with overt hostility, subtle slights, or passive-aggressive behavior, choosing to respond with tact and patience can prevent escalation and help you maintain your dignity and composure.

CAUSES OF RUDENESS (STRESS, PERSONALITY, CULTURAL DIFFERENCES)

Rudeness, whether intentional or not, is a common occurrence in many social and professional interactions. Understanding the causes of rudeness can help us respond in ways that defuse tension and maintain our composure. While we often react to rude behavior as if it were a personal attack, the reality is that rudeness can stem from a variety of factors that have little to do with the recipient. Three significant causes of rude behavior are stress, personality, and cultural differences. Each of these factors influences how people communicate and interact with others, often leading to misunderstandings or offensive behavior that is not always intentional.

Stress is one of the most common triggers of rude behavior. In today's fast-paced world, many individuals are under constant pressure to meet deadlines, achieve personal and professional goals, and manage numerous responsibilities. When stress levels rise, people can become short-tempered, irritable, and less able to manage their emotions. This can manifest as abrupt, rude, or dismissive behavior toward others, even when the person being rude may not consciously intend to offend.

For instance, imagine a manager who is juggling multiple projects with tight deadlines. Faced with the overwhelming pressure to deliver results, they might snap at an employee who asks a routine question, responding with impatience or even hostility. In this case, the rudeness is not necessarily a reflection of the employee's actions but rather an outward expression of the manager's internal stress. This type of behavior is often temporary and dissipates once the stressor is removed, but while it's happening, it can damage relationships and create a hostile work environment.

When people are under stress, their capacity for empathy and patience diminishes. They become more focused on their own problems and less attuned to the needs and feelings of others. This self-centered focus often leads to miscommunication, where someone might unintentionally come across as rude simply because they are too preoccupied with their own stress to consider how their words or actions are affecting others. Additionally, stress can lower one's tolerance for minor inconveniences or mistakes, making individuals more likely to react harshly to situations that they would normally handle with grace or patience.

Recognizing stress as a root cause of rudeness can help us respond more effectively. Instead of reacting defensively or taking the rudeness personally, it can be helpful to take a step back and consider whether the person may be under pressure. In many cases, offering a supportive or understanding response—rather than escalating the situation—can help defuse tension. For example, responding with empathy, such as saying, "It seems like things are really busy for you right now—let me know if I can help," can shift the dynamic from one of confrontation to one of mutual support.

Personality is another key factor that influences whether someone behaves rudely. While stress is often a temporary condition that can make even typically polite individuals behave in ways they normally wouldn't, personality traits tend to be more stable over time and are a significant predictor of how someone interacts with others. Some people are naturally more abrasive, blunt, or dismissive, not because they are under stress, but because it is simply part of their personality.

For example, individuals who exhibit traits associated with dominance, assertiveness, or low agreeableness may come across as rude or insensitive in their communication style. These individuals tend to be more focused on achieving their goals or asserting their opinions than on maintaining harmony or being considerate of others' feelings. While they may not intend to be hurtful, their directness and lack of social finesse can be perceived as rudeness, especially in situations where tact and diplomacy are expected.

On the other end of the spectrum, some people may engage in rude behavior because they are highly self-centered or have narcissistic tendencies. These individuals often place their own needs and desires above those of others, leading them to behave in ways that are dismissive, arrogant, or entitled. For example, a person with a strong sense of entitlement might feel justified in speaking down to others or interrupting conversations because they believe their time or opinions are more valuable than those of others. In these cases, the rudeness is not necessarily caused by an external factor, such as stress, but rather by deeply ingrained personality traits.

It's also important to recognize that some individuals may lack the social awareness or emotional intelligence to recognize when their behavior is rude. They may not pick up on subtle social cues or understand the impact of their words and actions on others. This lack of awareness can lead to frequent misunderstandings, where the person being rude is genuinely surprised to learn that their behavior was offensive. In such cases, offering constructive feedback in a respectful manner can help the individual become more conscious of how they come across to others.

While personality traits are relatively stable, people can learn to modify their behavior through self-awareness and social feedback. However, dealing with someone whose rudeness is tied to their personality can be challenging, as their behavior may not change easily. In these situations, it's often best to manage expectations and set clear boundaries. For example, if a colleague is known for being blunt or dismissive, it may be helpful to mentally prepare for such interactions and avoid taking their behavior personally. By focusing on the content of their message rather than the delivery, you can navigate the interaction without letting their personality traits affect your emotional well-being.

Cultural differences are another significant factor that can contribute to perceptions of rudeness. What is considered polite or appropriate behavior in one culture may be seen as rude or offensive in another. These differences can lead to misunderstandings and misinterpretations, especially in increasingly diverse workplaces and social environments. People from different cultural backgrounds often have different expectations regarding communication styles, personal space, eye contact, and even the use of silence, all of which can affect how their behavior is perceived.

For example, in some cultures, direct communication is valued, and people are expected to speak their minds openly, even if it involves delivering criticism or disagreeing with others. In these cultures, being straightforward is seen as a sign of honesty and respect. However, in cultures that place a higher value on indirect communication and maintaining harmony, this directness can come across as rude or confrontational. A person from a direct communication culture might give feedback like, "This report is full of errors—you need to fix it," while someone from a more indirect communication culture might say, "There are a few areas in the report that could be improved—perhaps you could review it again." The first statement, though intended to be efficient and clear, could be perceived as unnecessarily harsh or rude by someone who is used to a more diplomatic approach.

Similarly, cultural norms regarding personal space and physical touch can vary widely. In some cultures, it is common to stand close to others during conversations or to greet people with a handshake or even a kiss on the cheek. In other cultures, people may prefer more physical distance and view such gestures as intrusive or disrespectful. If someone unfamiliar with these cultural norms stands too close or touches another person in a way that feels inappropriate, it can easily be perceived as rude, even though the intention may have been to show warmth or friendliness.

Eye contact is another area where cultural differences can lead to misunderstandings. In some cultures, maintaining eye contact is seen as a sign of respect, confidence, and engagement, while in others, prolonged eye contact can be interpreted as aggressive or confrontational. Similarly, silence during a conversation might be viewed as awkward or uncomfortable in one culture, while in another, it could be seen as a natural part of the communication process, allowing for reflection and thoughtfulness.

Navigating cultural differences requires a high degree of cultural sensitivity and awareness. It's important to recognize that what may seem rude from one cultural perspective may be perfectly acceptable or even polite in another. Taking the time to learn about different cultural norms and communication styles can help prevent misunderstandings and foster more positive interactions in diverse environments. Additionally, when cultural differences lead to perceived rudeness, it's often helpful to approach the situation with curiosity rather than judgment. For example, if someone behaves in a way that feels rude or inappropriate, you might ask them about their cultural background or norms, which can open the door to a more meaningful and respectful exchange.

Understanding the causes of rudeness—whether it stems from stress, personality traits, or cultural differences—can help us respond with empathy, patience, and tact. By recognizing that rude behavior is not always a personal attack and may be influenced by factors beyond our control, we can approach these situations with a greater sense of composure and professionalism. Whether dealing with a stressed colleague, a personality clash, or a cultural misunderstanding, learning to navigate rude behavior effectively can improve relationships, reduce conflict, and create a more harmonious and respectful environment.

CHAPTER 1

THE IMPACT OF RUDENESS

EMOTIONAL TOLL ON THE RECIPIENT

Rudeness can be emotionally draining, especially when it occurs repeatedly or in environments where one feels vulnerable, such as at work. The emotional toll on the recipient of rude behavior often goes beyond the immediate discomfort of the moment. It can affect self-esteem, mental well-being, productivity, and even physical health. Understanding how this emotional burden manifests is crucial for anyone who finds themselves on the receiving end of rude behavior, as well as for those who wish to create a more respectful and supportive environment.

One of the most immediate effects of rudeness is the hit to self-esteem and confidence. When someone is treated rudely, especially in a professional setting, it can cause the recipient to question their abilities or worth. Comments or behaviors that belittle, dismiss, or disrespect another person may seem trivial to the perpetrator, but they can leave a lasting impression on the individual who experiences them. For instance, if a colleague constantly interrupts you during meetings, dismisses your ideas, or speaks to you in a condescending tone, it can create a sense of inadequacy. Over time, you may begin to internalize these negative interactions, doubting your competence or feeling unworthy of respect.

This erosion of self-esteem is particularly damaging in professional environments where confidence is closely tied to performance. A person who feels undermined or disrespected may become less likely to speak up in meetings, less confident in sharing ideas, and less willing to take risks, all of which can stifle professional growth and limit opportunities for advancement. The emotional weight of constantly questioning oneself can lead to feelings of helplessness, frustration, and even resentment. Over time, these emotions can accumulate, making it difficult to maintain a positive outlook or stay motivated in the face of ongoing rudeness.

The psychological effects of rudeness are not limited to self-doubt and diminished confidence. Rudeness also creates emotional stress, which can have a profound impact on mental health. When people are treated rudely, their bodies often respond with the same fight-or-flight reactions that occur in the face of physical threats. Their heart rate increases, stress hormones like cortisol are released, and they may feel tense, anxious, or angry. This physiological response can be particularly intense in situations where the recipient feels powerless to respond, such as when the rude behavior comes from someone in a position of authority.

Chronic exposure to rude behavior can lead to prolonged stress, which can manifest in a variety of ways. Individuals may experience difficulty concentrating, trouble sleeping, or mood swings. Anxiety and depression are also common outcomes of enduring disrespectful or demeaning interactions over an extended period. For some, the stress caused by rude behavior may spill over into other areas of life, affecting personal relationships or diminishing overall life satisfaction. This emotional strain can make it difficult to maintain a healthy work-life balance, as the feelings generated by rude encounters often linger long after the interaction has ended.

Moreover, rudeness can create a toxic environment that fosters negative emotions and diminishes morale. When rude behavior goes unchecked in a workplace, it can create a culture where disrespect becomes the norm. This can have a ripple effect, not only on the person who directly experiences the rude behavior but also on others who witness it. People may begin to feel less safe or supported in the workplace, leading to a decline in overall morale. They may also feel more isolated, as rudeness often erodes trust and cooperation among colleagues.

The emotional toll of this toxic environment is profound. In addition to feelings of stress, anxiety, and depression, recipients of rude behavior often experience feelings of loneliness or alienation. When people feel disrespected or undervalued, they may begin to withdraw from social interactions, both in the workplace and in their personal lives. This withdrawal can exacerbate feelings of isolation, as the individual becomes less engaged and more disconnected from their peers or support networks. The sense of alienation can also affect teamwork and collaboration, as individuals may become less willing to engage with others or share their ideas, fearing further disrespect or dismissal.

The emotional impact of rudeness is not always immediately visible, but its long-term effects can be devastating. Over time, recipients of rude behavior may develop a sense of emotional exhaustion or burnout. This state of emotional depletion occurs when the stress and negativity associated with rude interactions become too much to bear. Burnout is often characterized by feelings of hopelessness, detachment, and a lack of motivation. In extreme cases, it can lead individuals to disengage from their work entirely, either mentally or physically, as they become unable to cope with the ongoing emotional strain.

Another significant emotional consequence of rudeness is the toll it takes on interpersonal relationships. When someone is treated rudely, they may struggle to trust others or form meaningful connections. This can be particularly damaging in professional environments where collaboration and teamwork are essential. If someone feels that their contributions are consistently undervalued or that they are being disrespected by colleagues or supervisors, it can create a barrier to building positive working relationships. The person may become more guarded, less willing to share ideas, or less inclined to seek out opportunities for collaboration.

In personal relationships, the emotional toll of rudeness can lead to increased tension and conflict. Individuals who experience rudeness at work may carry the emotional burden home with them, where it affects their interactions with family members, friends, or romantic partners. Feelings of frustration, anger, or inadequacy can spill over into these relationships, causing misunderstandings or conflicts that might not have otherwise occurred. This emotional crossover from work to home life can exacerbate feelings of stress and strain, making it even more difficult to cope with rude behavior in the workplace.

Additionally, rude behavior often triggers feelings of anger or resentment in the recipient. While these emotions are natural and understandable, they can be difficult to manage, especially in professional settings where expressing anger openly may not be appropriate or possible. Suppressing these emotions can lead to emotional buildup, where the individual feels increasingly tense or on edge. Over time, this emotional buildup can manifest in unhealthy ways, such as irritability, passive-aggressive behavior, or even physical symptoms like headaches or muscle tension.

Managing the emotional toll of rudeness requires a high degree of emotional intelligence and resilience. It's important for recipients of rude behavior to recognize the impact that these interactions are having on their emotional well-being and to take steps to address the stress and negativity they are experiencing. This might involve practicing mindfulness techniques, seeking support from trusted colleagues or mentors, or finding healthy outlets for processing difficult emotions, such as journaling, exercise, or meditation.

In some cases, it may be necessary to set boundaries with individuals who consistently behave rudely or disrespectfully. While this can be challenging, especially when the rude behavior comes from someone in a position of power, it is essential for protecting one's emotional health. Setting boundaries might involve calmly addressing the behavior with the individual, letting them know how their actions are affecting you, or seeking support from a manager or HR representative if the behavior continues.

It's also important to cultivate self-compassion and not internalize the rude behavior of others. People who are treated rudely often blame themselves, wondering if they did something to provoke the behavior or if they are somehow deserving of disrespect. However, rudeness is usually a reflection of the other person's state of mind, not a statement about your worth or competence. By reminding yourself of this and practicing self-compassion, you can begin to shield yourself from the emotional toll of rude interactions and maintain your sense of self-worth.

Ultimately, the emotional toll of rudeness can have far-reaching consequences if left unchecked. It can undermine confidence, create chronic stress, damage relationships, and lead to burnout. However, by understanding the emotional impact of rude behavior and taking proactive steps to manage it, individuals can protect their emotional well-being and navigate difficult interactions with grace and resilience. While rudeness may be an inevitable part of life, the way we respond to it can determine whether it leaves a lasting negative impact or becomes an opportunity for growth and self-preservation.

NEGATIVE EFFECTS ON WORKPLACE MORALE AND PRODUCTIVITY

Rude behavior in the workplace, whether from colleagues, managers, or clients, can have a profound negative impact on both morale and productivity. When rudeness becomes a recurring issue, it erodes the sense of respect and cooperation that is essential for a healthy, functioning work environment. While an isolated rude comment may seem insignificant, its cumulative effects can create a toxic culture that affects the well-being of individuals and the performance of teams. Understanding how rudeness undermines morale and disrupts productivity is crucial for addressing the issue effectively and ensuring a more harmonious and productive workplace.

One of the most immediate effects of rudeness is the decline in workplace morale. Morale refers to the overall sense of satisfaction, motivation, and emotional well-being among employees. When morale is high, employees are typically more engaged, enthusiastic, and committed to their work. They feel valued and respected, which motivates them to contribute positively to the organization. However, when rudeness becomes prevalent, it erodes the sense of camaraderie and mutual respect that underpins strong morale.

Rude behavior can take many forms, from overt disrespect such as shouting or belittling comments to more subtle actions like dismissiveness, sarcasm, or exclusion. Regardless of its form, rudeness sends a clear message that the recipient is not valued or respected. Over time, this can lead to feelings of resentment, frustration, and alienation. Employees who feel disrespected may become disengaged, withdrawing emotionally from their work and their colleagues. This disengagement can spread throughout a team, as employees who witness rude behavior may also begin to feel demoralized, even if they are not directly targeted. They may question the fairness of their work environment or fear that they could be the next victim of rudeness.

When morale suffers, so too does teamwork. A healthy workplace thrives on collaboration, trust, and open communication. Employees need to feel comfortable sharing ideas, asking questions, and offering feedback without fear of being ridiculed or dismissed. However, when rudeness is present, it stifles open communication. Employees may become hesitant to speak up in meetings, fearing that their contributions will be met with sarcasm or condescension. This reluctance to engage in dialogue limits the exchange of ideas and creativity, which are essential for problem-solving and innovation.

Rudeness also creates an atmosphere of mistrust and competition rather than cooperation. Employees who experience or witness rude behavior may begin to adopt a more defensive or guarded stance, protecting themselves from potential attacks. This defensive attitude can make it difficult for teams to function cohesively, as individuals become more focused on self-preservation than on achieving common goals. In the worst cases, rudeness can escalate into conflicts or power struggles, further damaging relationships and creating divisions within the team. The result is a fragmented workplace where collaboration breaks down, and employees are less willing to help one another or work toward shared objectives.

The negative impact of rudeness on morale also extends to employees' sense of job satisfaction. Job satisfaction is closely linked to how employees feel about their work environment, their relationships with colleagues, and their sense of accomplishment. When employees are treated rudely, they may begin to dread coming to work, viewing it as a hostile or unfriendly place. This shift in perception can lead to a decline in job satisfaction, as employees feel less appreciated and more disconnected from their work. In turn, this can lead to increased absenteeism, as employees may try to avoid the negative environment by taking more sick days or arriving late to work.

Over time, low morale caused by rudeness can lead to higher turnover rates. Employees who feel consistently disrespected or undervalued are more likely to seek employment elsewhere, where they believe they will be treated with more respect and appreciation. High turnover is costly for organizations, both in terms of lost talent and the resources required to recruit and train new employees. Additionally, the loss of experienced employees can disrupt workflows and create knowledge gaps, further diminishing productivity.

The effects of rudeness on productivity are just as detrimental as its impact on morale. Productivity in the workplace relies on employees' ability to focus, work efficiently, and collaborate effectively. Rudeness disrupts this dynamic by introducing tension, stress, and distraction into the work environment. When employees are treated rudely, their ability to concentrate on tasks often diminishes. Instead of focusing on their work, they may spend time ruminating on the rude interaction, replaying it in their minds, and trying to make sense of what happened. This mental distraction can lead to decreased efficiency, as employees struggle to complete tasks while dealing with the emotional aftermath of rudeness.

Rudeness also contributes to stress, which has a direct impact on productivity. When employees are subjected to rude behavior, their stress levels increase. Stress triggers the body's fight-or-flight response, which can make it difficult to think clearly, make decisions, or perform tasks accurately. In high-stress environments where rudeness is frequent, employees may become more prone to errors, as their cognitive resources are diverted toward managing their stress rather than focusing on their work. This decline in performance can create a vicious cycle, where stressed employees make mistakes, leading to further criticism or rudeness, which in turn exacerbates their stress.

In addition to reducing individual productivity, rudeness can slow down team performance. As mentioned earlier, rudeness undermines collaboration by fostering mistrust and disengagement. When team members are reluctant to communicate openly or share ideas, projects may take longer to complete, and the quality of the work may suffer. Misunderstandings or miscommunications caused by rudeness can also lead to delays, as employees may be hesitant to ask for clarification or address issues that arise during the course of a project. This reluctance to engage can result in costly mistakes or missed opportunities for improvement, further decreasing overall productivity.

Another way that rudeness affects productivity is by damaging employee morale to the point where they become disengaged from their work. Disengaged employees are those who do the bare minimum to get by, often because they no longer feel invested in the success of the organization or their own personal growth. Rudeness is a key driver of disengagement, as it makes employees feel undervalued and unimportant. When employees disengage, their productivity drops significantly. They may stop taking initiative, avoid taking on additional responsibilities, and put in less effort overall. In some cases, disengaged employees may even actively sabotage projects or slow down progress out of frustration or resentment.

In a workplace where rudeness goes unchecked, these productivity losses can accumulate over time, leading to a noticeable decline in overall performance. Deadlines may be missed, quality may decline, and employee output may drop as more and more individuals disengage from their work. This loss of productivity not only affects the immediate team but can also have ripple effects throughout the organization, as other departments or teams become affected by the delays and mistakes caused by rudeness-induced disengagement.

Furthermore, rudeness can negatively impact customer interactions, which can have a direct effect on the organization's bottom line. Employees who are subjected to rude behavior may struggle to maintain their composure or remain professional when dealing with clients or customers. The stress and frustration caused by rudeness can make it more difficult for employees to provide high-quality customer service, leading to negative customer experiences. In industries where customer satisfaction is critical, this decline in service quality can result in lost business, damaged reputations, and reduced revenue.

In some cases, rudeness can even escalate to workplace bullying, which has even more severe consequences for morale and productivity. Bullying creates a hostile work environment where employees feel unsafe, anxious, and demoralized. The emotional toll of workplace bullying can lead to severe mental health issues, such as anxiety, depression, or burnout, all of which further diminish productivity. Employees who are targeted by bullying or who witness bullying may become increasingly disengaged and stressed, further contributing to the decline in morale and productivity across the organization.

Addressing rudeness in the workplace is essential for maintaining a positive, productive environment. Organizations that fail to address rude behavior risk creating a toxic culture where low morale, disengagement, and decreased productivity become the norm. To combat this, it's important to create a culture of respect, where rudeness is not tolerated, and where employees feel supported and valued. This can be achieved through clear policies that outline expectations for respectful behavior, as well as training programs that teach employees how to communicate effectively and resolve conflicts in a professional manner.

Leadership also plays a critical role in mitigating the negative effects of rudeness on morale and productivity. Leaders set the tone for the organization, and their behavior serves as a model for how employees should interact with one another. When leaders demonstrate respect, empathy, and professionalism in their interactions, it creates a culture where rudeness is less likely to thrive. Conversely, when leaders engage in or tolerate rude behavior, it signals to employees that such behavior is acceptable, further perpetuating the cycle of low morale and decreased productivity.

Rudeness has far-reaching consequences that extend beyond the individual who experiences it. It diminishes morale, undermines collaboration, and disrupts productivity, creating a work environment where employees feel disengaged, stressed, and undervalued. Addressing rudeness and fostering a culture of respect is essential for maintaining a positive, productive workplace where employees can thrive and contribute their best efforts.

LEGAL IMPLICATIONS OF WORKPLACE HARASSMENT

Workplace harassment is a significant issue with serious legal implications that can affect both employees and employers. Harassment, when left unchecked, creates a toxic environment that not only damages relationships and morale but also exposes companies to substantial legal risks. Understanding the legal implications of workplace harassment is essential for preventing it, addressing it effectively, and ensuring compliance with employment laws. Both employees and employers must recognize the potential consequences of harassment, including legal liability, fines, and damage to the company's reputation.

Workplace harassment is typically defined as any unwanted behavior that creates a hostile, intimidating, or offensive work environment for one or more individuals. This can include actions such as verbal abuse, physical intimidation, or inappropriate jokes, as well as more subtle forms of mistreatment, like exclusion or belittling comments. Harassment often involves a misuse of power or authority, but it can also occur between colleagues of equal status. While it may sometimes be dismissed as just part of workplace dynamics, harassment can rise to the level of a legal violation if it is based on certain protected characteristics or if it becomes pervasive enough to interfere with the victim's ability to work.

Harassment becomes illegal under employment law when it is based on characteristics that are protected by anti-discrimination laws. These characteristics typically include race, color, religion, sex, national origin, age, disability, and in some cases, sexual orientation or gender identity. In many countries, including the United States, the law prohibits harassment on these grounds under civil rights legislation. For example, in the U.S., Title VII of the Civil Rights Act of 1964 makes it illegal to harass someone based on their race, sex, or religion, among other categories. Similarly, the Americans with Disabilities Act (ADA) protects employees with disabilities from harassment, and the Age Discrimination in Employment Act (ADEA) offers protections for workers over 40 years of age.

Sexual harassment, in particular, has gained widespread attention and is often the focus of workplace harassment laws. Sexual harassment can involve unwelcome advances, requests for sexual favors, or other verbal or physical conduct of a sexual nature. It is illegal when it affects an individual's employment, interferes with their work performance, or creates a hostile or intimidating work environment. The law recognizes two main types of sexual harassment: quid pro quo harassment and hostile work environment harassment. Quid pro quo harassment occurs when a supervisor or person in authority makes submission to sexual advances a condition for employment decisions, such as promotions or raises. Hostile work environment harassment occurs when the behavior is so severe or pervasive that it alters the conditions of employment, making the workplace unbearable for the victim.

The legal implications of harassment extend beyond just sexual harassment, however. Harassment based on race, national origin, or religion can also have profound legal consequences. For instance, racial harassment might include offensive comments, slurs, or jokes targeting a person's race or ethnicity, while religious harassment might involve mocking someone's religious beliefs or practices. These behaviors not only violate moral and ethical standards but also breach anti-discrimination laws that seek to ensure equal treatment in the workplace. Employers who fail to address these issues can face legal action, including lawsuits, settlements, and punitive damages.

The legal framework surrounding workplace harassment also extends to retaliation. It is illegal for employers to retaliate against employees who report harassment or participate in investigations into harassment claims. Retaliation can take many forms, such as demotions, pay cuts, undesirable job assignments, or even termination. Retaliation claims are common in harassment cases and are treated seriously by courts. Employees who experience retaliation have legal grounds to file complaints or lawsuits, and employers found guilty of retaliation may face significant financial penalties, including back pay, reinstatement of the employee, or compensatory damages for emotional distress.

Employers have a legal obligation to prevent harassment and to take prompt, effective action when it occurs. This includes creating and enforcing policies that prohibit harassment, providing training to employees and supervisors, and establishing clear procedures for reporting and investigating complaints. Many countries require employers to take reasonable steps to prevent harassment, and failure to do so can result in legal liability. If an employee files a harassment complaint and the employer does not investigate the claim adequately or fails to take corrective action, the employer can be held legally responsible for allowing the harassment to continue. This is especially true if the harassment comes from someone in a supervisory role, as employers are typically held to a higher standard of accountability when managers or executives are involved.

In some cases, employers may be held vicariously liable for the actions of their employees. This means that even if the employer was not directly involved in the harassment, they can still be legally responsible for thc behavior of their employees if it occurs within the scope of their employment. For example, if a manager harasses a subordinate and the employer knew or should have known about the behavior but failed to stop it, the employer can be held liable. Courts often look at whether the employer had appropriate policies in place and whether they responded appropriately to complaints of harassment when determining liability.

Workplace harassment can lead to costly legal battles that result in large settlements or judgments. In recent years, high profile harassment cases have led to multi-million dollar settlements for victims. These legal costs can be devastating for companies, not only financially but also in terms of reputational damage. Companies that are sued for workplace harassment may find it difficult to attract and retain top talent, as prospective employees may be wary of working for a company with a history of harassment issues. Additionally, the negative publicity surrounding harassment lawsuits can lead to a loss of business, as clients and customers may choose to take their business elsewhere.

Beyond the financial costs, harassment can have serious personal consequences for the individuals involved. Victims of harassment often suffer from emotional and psychological distress, which can lead to anxiety, depression, and even post-traumatic stress disorder (PTSD). In some cases, victims may need to take time off work to recover, leading to lost wages and additional financial hardship. Harassment can also affect victims' careers, as they may feel forced to leave their jobs to escape the hostile environment, potentially losing opportunities for advancement and professional development.

For employers, addressing harassment effectively is not just a legal requirement but a moral imperative. Organizations that fail to take workplace harassment seriously risk creating a culture of fear, mistrust, and resentment, which can severely undermine employee morale and productivity. Employers must be proactive in fostering a respectful and inclusive work environment where employees feel safe and supported. This requires a commitment to diversity, equity, and inclusion, as well as a willingness to confront and address inappropriate behavior, regardless of who is involved.

One of the key steps employers can take to prevent harassment is to provide regular training to employees and supervisors. This training should cover what constitutes harassment, how to recognize it, and what employees should do if they experience or witness it. Employees need to know that the company takes harassment seriously and that there are clear procedures in place for addressing complaints. Supervisors, in particular, should be trained on how to handle harassment complaints and how to prevent retaliation. Many countries mandate workplace harassment training, and failure to provide such training can result in penalties or increased liability in harassment cases.

Employers should also create a clear, accessible reporting process for harassment complaints. Employees need to feel comfortable coming forward with complaints without fear of retaliation or dismissal. The reporting process should be confidential, and employers should respond promptly to complaints by conducting a thorough investigation. If harassment is found to have occurred, employers must take appropriate action to address the behavior, which may include disciplinary measures, reassignment, or termination of the offender. Employers should also provide support to the victim, such as counseling services or temporary adjustments to their work environment, to help them recover from the experience.

In addition to legal remedies, many countries have government agencies that enforce anti-harassment laws and provide resources for victims of harassment. In the United States, for example, the Equal Employment Opportunity Commission (EEOC) is responsible for investigating claims of workplace discrimination and harassment. Employees who believe they have been harassed can file a complaint with the EEOC, which will investigate the claim and attempt to resolve it through mediation or settlement. If the EEOC finds evidence of harassment, it may file a lawsuit on behalf of the employee or issue a "right to sue" letter, allowing the employee to pursue legal action independently.

In some cases, employees may choose to pursue civil litigation against their employers for harassment. This can result in a trial where a jury or judge will determine whether the employer is liable for the harassment and what damages should be awarded. Damages in harassment cases can include compensatory damages for lost wages, emotional distress, and punitive damages designed to punish the employer for egregious conduct. In many cases, employers choose to settle harassment claims out of court to avoid the cost and uncertainty of litigation, as well as the negative publicity that often accompanies a trial.

The legal implications of workplace harassment are significant and far-reaching. Employers must be vigilant in preventing harassment and addressing it promptly when it occurs, or they risk facing substantial legal and financial consequences. Harassment not only violates employees' rights but also damages the overall health of an organization. By fostering a culture of respect and inclusion, employers can reduce the risk of harassment and create a more positive, productive work environment for everyone.

PART II

Developing Tactful Responses

CHAPTER 2

THE POWER OF ACTIVE LISTENING

UNDERSTANDING THE OTHER PERSON'S PERSPECTIVE

Understanding the other person's perspective is a crucial skill in navigating difficult conversations, especially when dealing with rudeness. While it may seem counterintuitive to attempt to empathize with someone who has been disrespectful, this approach often offers significant benefits. First, it allows you to respond in a manner that is both tactful and effective, which can prevent further escalation and protect your professional relationships. Second, it fosters emotional intelligence, helping you develop resilience and patience in the face of challenging interpersonal dynamics. By taking the time to understand what might be motivating the other person's behavior, you increase your chances of responding thoughtfully rather than reactively, and you open up the possibility of resolving conflicts in a constructive way.

Rudeness can often stem from factors that have little to do with the immediate situation. Stress, personal frustrations, or even misunderstandings can fuel rude behavior. By attempting to look beyond the words or actions and considering what might be driving the behavior, you can create a more objective view of the situation. For example, if someone is short-tempered during a meeting, it's possible that they are dealing with overwhelming deadlines or personal issues outside of work. This doesn't excuse rude behavior, but it helps you contextualize it and reduces the likelihood that you will take it personally. Understanding the other person's stressors can lead to more compassion in your responses, which in turn may diffuse their tension rather than inflame it.

Another key element of understanding someone else's perspective is recognizing that people have different communication styles. What one person considers rude may be a normal way of expressing frustration for another. Cultural differences also play a role in shaping how people communicate, and what may be perceived as rude in one culture might be seen as direct or straightforward in another. A person who speaks bluntly may not intend to cause offense; they may simply value efficiency and clarity over politeness. By acknowledging these differences, you can give the other person the benefit of the doubt and engage with them more thoughtfully. Rather than immediately assuming malice or disrespect, you can approach the situation with curiosity and a willingness to understand where they are coming from.

It's also important to realize that the rude behavior might be a reflection of the other person's own insecurities. Sometimes, people lash out because they feel threatened or inadequate in some way. In a work environment, for instance, a colleague might respond rudely if they perceive that their position is being challenged or if they feel overwhelmed by their workload. In these cases, understanding the root cause of their behavior can allow you to respond in a way that diffuses the situation rather than escalating it. You might choose to address the underlying issue directly, offering support or clarifying any misunderstandings that may be contributing to their sense of insecurity.

This approach also requires a degree of emotional regulation on your part. When someone is rude to you, your immediate instinct might be to defend yourself or respond in kind. However, by taking a moment to assess the situation and consider the other person's state of mind, you gain control over your response. This ability to pause and reflect is essential in preventing knee-jerk reactions that could escalate the situation. Understanding the other person's perspective helps you see that their behavior may not be a personal attack, but rather a reflection of their own struggles or frustrations.

By choosing to respond with patience and empathy, you not only maintain your composure but also set a positive example for others in the workplace.

It's important to note that understanding the other person's perspective doesn't mean excusing or condoning rude behavior. Empathy doesn't negate the need for boundaries. While you can acknowledge that someone might be dealing with personal issues or stress, this doesn't mean you have to accept or tolerate disrespect. What it does mean is that you are choosing to address the situation from a place of emotional intelligence. By approaching the person with understanding, you can set the stage for a more productive conversation. You might say something like, "I understand you're under a lot of pressure right now, but the way you addressed that issue felt disrespectful." This approach acknowledges their feelings while still holding them accountable for their behavior.

Understanding the other person's perspective also means recognizing that everyone has their own unique experiences and challenges that shape how they respond to stress. Perhaps the individual grew up in an environment where conflict was handled poorly, and they never learned how to express their frustration constructively. Or maybe they've faced discrimination or bias in the past, making them more sensitive to certain comments or actions. By keeping this in mind, you can approach difficult interactions with greater compassion and patience. It's possible that their rudeness isn't about you at all but is instead a reaction to their own internal struggles.

In some cases, understanding the other person's perspective can reveal that their rude behavior is a defense mechanism. People often use rudeness to mask vulnerability or to protect themselves from feeling exposed. If someone feels uncertain or inadequate, they might use sarcasm, dismissiveness, or aggression as a way to regain control of the situation. Recognizing this can help you avoid getting drawn into a power struggle. Instead of responding defensively, you can de-escalate the situation by remaining calm and addressing the underlying insecurity or fear that may be fueling their behavior. This doesn't mean you need to play the role of therapist, but it does mean you can respond with a level of understanding that helps diffuse tension.

Sometimes, understanding the other person's perspective requires active listening. Rudeness can often arise when people feel unheard or dismissed. If someone feels like their concerns are being ignored or belittled, they may resort to rude behavior as a way to assert themselves. By making a conscious effort to listen more attentively, you can often prevent this escalation. When someone feels that they are being truly heard, they are more likely to calm down and communicate their concerns in a more respectful manner. Active listening involves not only hearing the words the other person is saying but also picking up on the emotions behind those words. By acknowledging their feelings, you validate their experience, which can help reduce the tension in the interaction.

It's also helpful to understand that people's capacity to manage their emotions can vary greatly. Some individuals are naturally more emotionally regulated, while others may struggle to maintain composure under stress. When someone behaves rudely, it could be a sign that they are overwhelmed and unable to manage their emotions effectively in that moment. Understanding this can help you approach the situation with greater empathy, recognizing that the person may not have the tools or emotional resources to respond in a more appropriate way. This doesn't excuse their behavior, but it does help you maintain a sense of perspective, allowing you to respond in a way that is both firm and compassionate.

Understanding another person's perspective also involves recognizing that people often have different priorities and values. What seems important to you may not hold the same significance for someone else, and this mismatch can lead to frustration or miscommunication. For example, if a colleague is rude because they feel that you're not taking a project seriously, it could be because they value efficiency and results above all else. By acknowledging their priorities, you can adjust your communication to show that you understand and respect their concerns, even if you don't necessarily agree with them. This can help reduce friction and create a more collaborative working relationship.

Understanding the other person's perspective is about fostering connection and empathy. Even in the face of rude behavior, recognizing the humanity in the other person can shift the tone of the interaction. Everyone has moments of weakness, stress, and frustration, and remembering that the other person is dealing with their own challenges can help you approach the situation with kindness rather than defensiveness. By cultivating empathy, you not only improve your own emotional well-being but also create an environment where conflict is less likely to escalate and more likely to be resolved peacefully.

Understanding the other person's perspective is a powerful tool in managing difficult interactions. It allows you to approach rudeness with empathy and patience, helping you to respond in a way that is both respectful and effective. While it doesn't excuse bad behavior, it helps you see the situation in a broader context, which can prevent unnecessary conflict and lead to more productive conversations. By practicing empathy, active listening, and emotional regulation, you can navigate tricky situations with grace and maintain positive relationships, even in the face of rudeness.

EMPATHIZING WITHOUT CONDONING

Empathizing with someone who is rude without condoning their behavior is a delicate balancing act. It requires a blend of emotional intelligence, self-awareness, and a clear understanding of boundaries. Empathy involves the ability to understand and share the feelings of another person, putting yourself in their shoes to grasp what they might be experiencing or thinking. However, empathizing with someone doesn't mean that you automatically accept or excuse their behavior, especially if it is harmful, rude, or disrespectful. The key is to separate the person from their actions, recognizing their humanity while still maintaining your own boundaries and holding them accountable for their behavior.

At its core, empathy is about understanding rather than judgment. When someone behaves rudely, it is often the result of stress, frustration, or insecurity. By empathizing, you acknowledge that the person may be dealing with difficulties that are affecting their behavior, but this does not mean you have to accept the rudeness. You can recognize that someone is under pressure, for instance, while still maintaining that their tone or actions are inappropriate. This approach allows you to remain compassionate without becoming a doormat for bad behavior. It's a way of staying emotionally engaged while protecting yourself from unnecessary harm or disrespect.

One of the primary reasons people conflate empathy with condoning is that they believe understanding someone's feelings or circumstances makes their actions justifiable. In reality, empathizing with someone merely means you are attempting to understand their perspective, not that you agree with it. When dealing with rude people, this distinction becomes crucial. You can acknowledge that a colleague, for example, is overwhelmed with a heavy workload, and that this stress may have caused them to snap or act irritably. However, you can also assert that this does not give them the right to treat you or others disrespectfully. This kind of empathetic yet firm stance helps you maintain your own emotional boundaries while still offering compassion.

Empathy without condoning also involves clear communication. When you recognize that someone's rudeness stems from a deeper issue, such as stress or insecurity, you have the opportunity to address it constructively. You might say something like, "I can see that you're feeling overwhelmed right now, and I want to support you, but the way you're speaking to me feels disrespectful." This kind of response communicates empathy by acknowledging their feelings, but it also sets a boundary by calling out the inappropriate behavior. The ability to articulate both understanding and limits is essential in maintaining healthy professional and personal relationships, particularly when dealing with rude or difficult people.

In many cases, people may not even be aware that they are being rude, especially if they are caught up in their own stress or frustration. Empathizing with them can provide an opening for constructive dialogue, helping them reflect on their behavior without feeling attacked. By offering a measured response, you avoid escalating the situation and may even help the person recognize that their behavior was inappropriate. This can be particularly effective in workplace settings where maintaining positive relationships is crucial to productivity and morale. A tactful, empathetic response can turn a potentially confrontational moment into an opportunity for growth and mutual understanding.

Empathizing without condoning also involves managing your own emotions. When someone is rude to you, it's natural to feel hurt, angry, or defensive. However, reacting impulsively or matching their rudeness with your own can lead to further conflict. By pausing to consider the other person's perspective, you gain control over your emotional response. You can choose to react in a way that reflects your values and principles, rather than getting pulled into their negativity. This not only helps you maintain your composure but also demonstrates emotional maturity and self-control, both of which are essential in navigating tricky social or professional dynamics.

One of the benefits of empathizing without condoning is that it helps you protect your own emotional well-being.

When you empathize with someone, you are able to detach from the immediate emotional sting of their words or actions. Instead of personalizing the rudeness, you recognize that it may be a reflection of their internal struggles rather than something you've done wrong. This perspective allows you to maintain a sense of inner peace and self-assurance, even in the face of negative behavior. By understanding where the other person is coming from, you can choose to remain calm and centered, rather than getting caught up in the emotional whirlwind of the moment.

However, it's important to note that empathy without condoning doesn't mean allowing others to mistreat you. Maintaining your own boundaries is critical, and this means being able to assert yourself when necessary. Empathy is not about letting people walk all over you or excusing bad behavior. Rather, it's about understanding the reasons behind someone's actions while still holding them accountable. For example, if a colleague regularly speaks to you in a condescending tone, empathizing with their stress or frustration doesn't mean you have to accept their disrespect. You can still address the issue directly, expressing both your understanding of their situation and your need for more respectful communication moving forward.

In some cases, empathizing with someone can actually help them see the impact of their behavior in a way that defensiveness or confrontation would not. When people feel attacked or criticized, they are more likely to dig in their heels and defend their actions. However, when they feel understood, they may be more open to reflecting on how their behavior has affected others. By showing empathy, you create an environment where the other person feels safe enough to let down their guard and consider alternative ways of interacting. This can be a powerful tool for conflict resolution, particularly in professional settings where ongoing relationships are necessary.

That said, there are limits to empathy, and it's important to recognize when someone's behavior crosses the line into unacceptability. There are situations where rudeness becomes abuse or harassment, and in these cases, empathy should not be used as a justification to endure harmful behavior. In such instances, your priority must be to protect yourself, whether that means setting firmer boundaries, seeking support from management or HR, or, in extreme cases, removing yourself from the situation entirely. While empathy can be a valuable tool in navigating difficult interactions, it should never come at the expense of your own well-being or safety.

Empathizing without condoning also involves a level of self-reflection. It requires you to examine your own reactions and biases, ensuring that you are approaching the situation with an open mind. Sometimes, our own frustrations or stress can make us more sensitive to perceived rudeness, and it's important to recognize when we might be contributing to the tension. By checking in with ourselves and ensuring that we are not projecting our own emotions onto the situation, we can engage with others from a place of clarity and fairness. This self-awareness not only helps us navigate rude interactions but also fosters healthier, more productive relationships overall.

Practicing empathy without condoning is a skill that takes time and effort to develop. It requires patience, self-discipline, and a willingness to see beyond the surface of someone's behavior. However, the rewards are significant. By learning to empathize with others while maintaining your own boundaries, you can transform difficult interactions into opportunities for growth and connection. You can create an environment where people feel understood and respected, even in moments of conflict, and where accountability and compassion coexist. This balance is the foundation of effective communication and conflict resolution, allowing you to navigate tricky situations with grace and professionalism.

Empathizing with someone who is rude does not mean accepting or excusing their behavior. It means understanding the underlying causes of their actions while still maintaining your own boundaries and insisting on respectful communication. Empathy allows you to respond with compassion and emotional intelligence, helping to diffuse tension and create an opening for constructive dialogue. However, it also requires you to be clear about what behavior is acceptable and what is not, ensuring that you protect your own well-being while still engaging with others in a thoughtful and compassionate manner. By practicing empathy without condoning, you can handle difficult interactions with grace, maintaining both your professionalism and your emotional equilibrium.

CHAPTER 3
EFFECTIVE COMMUNICATION TECHNIQUES

"I" STATEMENTS: EXPRESSING FEELINGS WITHOUT BLAMING

One of the most effective communication tools for diffusing tension and preventing misunderstandings in difficult situations is the use of "I" statements. These statements allow you to express your feelings, needs, and concerns without blaming or attacking the other person. When used correctly, "I" statements help foster open dialogue, create understanding, and maintain respect between the parties involved. This is especially important when dealing with rude or confrontational behavior, where emotions can run high, and it's easy for conversations to become heated.

The primary goal of an "I" statement is to take ownership of your feelings and experiences without making the other person feel defensive. This stands in contrast to "you" statements, which often come across as accusatory and can quickly escalate conflict. For instance, saying "You're always so rude!" immediately puts the other person on the defensive, making it more likely that they will respond with hostility. In contrast, an "I" statement such as "I feel disrespected when you speak to me in that tone" shifts the focus away from the other person's actions and centers on your own feelings. This invites the other person to listen without feeling attacked and opens the door for more constructive communication.

At the heart of an "I" statement is the expression of your feelings in a clear and non-confrontational way. It's a way of saying, "This is how I feel in response to what is happening," rather than, "This is what you are doing wrong."

This distinction is important because it acknowledges that your feelings are your own and that they are valid, without assigning blame or making assumptions about the other person's intentions. This is particularly helpful in tense or emotionally charged situations, where it's easy to assume that the other person is deliberately trying to upset or provoke you. By focusing on your feelings rather than their actions, you can communicate your emotional experience without escalating the conflict.

Another important aspect of "I" statements is that they provide an opportunity for self-reflection. When you take the time to craft an "I" statement, you are forced to think about your own emotions and why you are feeling the way you do. This can prevent you from reacting impulsively or saying something you might later regret. For example, instead of immediately lashing out in response to a rude comment, you might pause to consider what it is about the comment that bothered you. You may realize that you felt disrespected or undervalued, and this self-awareness can help you communicate your feelings in a more thoughtful and measured way.

In addition to expressing feelings, "I" statements can also include a description of the specific behavior or situation that led to those feelings. This helps the other person understand the context of your emotions without feeling blamed. For example, instead of saying, "You never listen to me," which is likely to provoke a defensive response, you could say, "I feel frustrated when I'm not able to finish my thoughts in conversations." This statement focuses on your emotional experience and provides a clear explanation of what caused it, without accusing the other person of wrongdoing. By focusing on the specific behavior rather than attacking the person's character, you increase the chances of the other person being receptive to your concerns.

Moreover, "I" statements can help clarify misunderstandings and prevent miscommunication. In many cases, people may not even realize that their behavior is having a negative impact on others. By using an "I" statement, you provide the other person with valuable insight into how their actions are affecting you. This can be especially important in professional settings, where clear communication is essential for maintaining a positive work environment. For instance, if a colleague consistently interrupts you during meetings, you might say, "I feel unheard when I'm interrupted before I can finish my point." This not only expresses your feelings but also highlights the specific behavior that is causing the issue, giving the other person a clear understanding of what needs to change.

"I" statements also have the benefit of encouraging empathy and cooperation. When you express your feelings in a non-confrontational way, the other person is more likely to respond with understanding rather than defensiveness. This can help create a more collaborative atmosphere, where both parties feel heard and respected. In contrast, "you" statements often shut down dialogue by making the other person feel attacked or blamed. By focusing on your own feelings and experiences, you invite the other person to empathize with your perspective and work with you to find a solution.

Furthermore, "I" statements are an important tool for setting boundaries in a respectful and assertive way. Setting boundaries is essential for maintaining healthy relationships, both personally and professionally, and "I" statements allow you to communicate your limits without coming across as aggressive or confrontational. For example, if a coworker frequently makes sarcastic comments that you find hurtful, you might say, "I feel uncomfortable when jokes are made at my expense." This clearly communicates your discomfort while avoiding accusations or blame, making it more likely that the other person will respect your boundaries without feeling attacked.

It's also important to remember that "I" statements are not about controlling the other person's behavior but about expressing your own needs and feelings. While you can't control how someone else will react or whether they will change their behavior, you can control how you communicate your emotions and assert your boundaries. "I" statements empower you to take ownership of your own feelings and advocate for yourself in a way that is both respectful and effective. They allow you to express your needs without resorting to blame or accusations, which can help prevent conflicts from escalating and promote more positive and productive interactions.

One of the challenges of using "I" statements is that it can feel vulnerable to express your emotions so directly. In many cases, people are hesitant to share their feelings because they fear being dismissed, misunderstood, or seen as weak. However, vulnerability is an essential part of building trust and fostering healthy communication. When you use an "I" statement, you are not only expressing your feelings but also demonstrating a willingness to engage in open and honest dialogue. This can help build stronger, more authentic relationships, where both parties feel comfortable expressing their needs and working together to resolve conflicts.

It's worth noting that "I" statements are not a magic solution to all communication challenges. There will be times when the other person may still react defensively or refuse to engage constructively, despite your best efforts. However, by using "I" statements, you are doing your part to communicate in a way that is respectful, clear, and non-confrontational. This can help de-escalate tension and create a more positive atmosphere, even in difficult situations. Additionally, by consistently using "I" statements, you set a positive example for others, demonstrating the value of taking responsibility for your own emotions and communicating assertively without blame.

To effectively use "I" statements, it's important to bc mindful of your tone and body language. Even the most well-crafted "I" statement can come across as accusatory if delivered with a harsh or condescending tone. Similarly, defensive body language, such as crossing your arms or avoiding eye contact, can undermine the message you're trying to convey. When using "I" statements, aim for a calm, measured tone and open body language that invites dialogue rather than confrontation. This will help ensure that your message is received in the spirit in which it was intended and increase the likelihood of a positive response.

"I" statements are a powerful tool for expressing feelings without blaming, promoting healthy communication, and resolving conflicts in a constructive way. By focusing on your own emotions and experiences, you can communicate your needs and concerns without making the other person feel attacked or defensive. This not only helps prevent misunderstandings and miscommunication but also fosters empathy, cooperation, and mutual respect. While using "I" statements requires practice and self-awareness, the benefits are well worth the effort, particularly in challenging situations where emotions can easily run high. By mastering the art of "I" statements, you can navigate difficult conversations with confidence, assertiveness, and grace, ultimately leading to more positive and productive interactions.

ASSERTIVE COMMUNICATION: STANDING UP FOR ONESELF RESPECTFULLY

Assertive communication is one of the most powerful tools in any interpersonal interaction, especially when faced with challenging or rude behavior. It represents a balanced and confident way of expressing your thoughts, needs, and feelings while respecting the rights and perspectives of others. The ability to stand up for oneself respectfully, without aggression or passivity, can dramatically improve relationships, resolve conflicts, and enhance self-esteem. While it's easy to confuse assertiveness with aggression, true assertiveness creates an environment where open dialogue and mutual respect are encouraged, fostering better understanding and cooperation.

At its core, assertive communication allows individuals to express themselves openly and honestly, stating their desires and opinions without diminishing the feelings of others. It's about advocating for your own rights while simultaneously respecting the rights of the person you are engaging with. In contrast, aggressive communication disregards the needs and feelings of others, focusing solely on one's own desires. Passive communication, on the other hand, involves suppressing one's own needs to avoid confrontation, often leading to resentment and frustration. Assertiveness finds the middle ground, enabling individuals to stand up for themselves in a way that promotes both self-respect and respect for others.

The importance of assertiveness becomes particularly evident in difficult or stressful interactions, such as when dealing with rude people. In these moments, it's tempting to respond either aggressively, meeting rudeness with more hostility, or passively, allowing the rude behavior to continue unchallenged. However, neither approach leads to a positive outcome. Aggressive responses may escalate the situation, causing further tension and damaging relationships, while passive responses can enable disrespectful behavior to persist. Assertive communication, on the other hand, offers a way to address the issue directly without creating further conflict. It allows you to stand your ground, express your boundaries, and maintain your self-respect without belittling or attacking the other person.

One key aspect of assertive communication is clarity. When standing up for yourself, it's important to be clear and specific about what you want or how you feel. Vague or ambiguous statements can lead to misunderstandings, leaving the other person unsure of what you are asking for or why you are upset. For example, instead of saying "You're being rude," a more assertive approach would be, "I find it disrespectful when you interrupt me while I'm speaking." This not only clearly communicates the behavior that is causing the issue but also conveys your feelings in a way that is non-confrontational and focused on resolution.

Assertive communication also involves using calm and neutral language. Even when addressing difficult behavior, it's important to avoid inflammatory words or a harsh tone, as these can quickly escalate the situation. The goal is not to make the other person feel attacked or defensive but to express your needs in a way that is firm yet respectful. A calm, measured tone, coupled with polite but direct language, signals that you are serious about your boundaries while still being open to dialogue. For example, instead of raising your voice or using sarcasm in response to a rude comment, you could calmly say, "I would appreciate it if we could keep this conversation respectful." This assertive approach communicates your expectations without creating further animosity.

In addition to verbal communication, assertiveness is reflected in non-verbal cues. Body language, facial expressions, and eye contact all play a crucial role in conveying assertiveness. Standing or sitting upright, making appropriate eye contact, and maintaining a neutral but attentive facial expression all contribute to a confident yet respectful demeanor. Slouched posture or avoidance of eye contact can send the message that you are unsure of yourself, while overly aggressive body language, such as pointing or invading the other person's personal space, can come across as confrontational. Assertive body language strikes a balance, projecting confidence without aggression, and helps reinforce the message that you are standing up for yourself in a respectful manner.

Another fundamental element of assertive communication is the ability to say no without guilt. Many people struggle with setting boundaries, especially in situations where they feel pressured to please others or avoid conflict. However, assertiveness involves recognizing that it's okay to say no when something doesn't align with your values, needs, or priorities. Saying no assertively does not mean being rude or dismissive; rather, it's about being clear and firm in your refusal while maintaining respect for the other person. For instance, if a colleague asks you to take on extra work that you simply don't have the capacity to handle, you might say, "I'm unable to take on more work at this time, but I can help you find someone else who may be able to assist." This response is direct and respectful, asserting your boundaries while offering a possible solution.

Listening is another critical component of assertive communication. Being assertive is not just about expressing your own needs; it's also about being open to hearing the other person's perspective. Active listening shows that you value the other person's viewpoint, even if you don't agree with it, and can help diffuse tension in a difficult conversation. When someone feels heard, they are more likely to respond positively, even in situations where there is disagreement. Listening actively, maintaining eye contact, and responding thoughtfully to what the other person is saying can foster a more collaborative and respectful exchange. By engaging in a two-way conversation rather than simply asserting your own needs, you create space for mutual understanding and problem-solving.

In challenging situations, especially when dealing with rude or disrespectful behavior, it can be difficult to remain assertive without veering into aggression or passivity. One effective technique for maintaining assertiveness is to focus on the issue at hand, rather than attacking the other person's character. For example, instead of saying, "You're always so inconsiderate," you could say, "I felt frustrated when the project wasn't completed on time, as it affected my ability to meet my own deadlines." This shifts the focus from blaming the other person to addressing the specific issue that is causing the conflict. By focusing on the behavior rather than the person, you can communicate your feelings without escalating the situation.

Another technique for assertive communication is to use "I" statements, which allow you to express your feelings and needs without sounding accusatory. For instance, instead of saying, “You never listen to me,” which might make the other person defensive, you could say, “I feel unheard when I’m interrupted during meetings.” This keeps the conversation focused on your personal experience, making it less likely to provoke a negative reaction. "I" statements also demonstrate that you are taking responsibility for your own emotions, rather than placing the blame entirely on the other person. This can encourage a more open and constructive conversation, where both parties feel heard and respected.

Remaining assertive in the face of rude behavior also requires emotional regulation. It’s natural to feel upset or frustrated when someone is disrespectful, but reacting impulsively can lead to an aggressive or passive response. Taking a moment to pause, breathe, and reflect on your feelings before responding can help you maintain your composure and communicate assertively. Emotional regulation allows you to approach the situation with a calm and clear mind, making it easier to articulate your needs and boundaries without losing your temper or retreating into passivity. It also shows the other person that you are in control of your emotions, which can help de-escalate the situation and foster more respectful communication.

In situations where assertiveness is necessary, it’s also important to remain consistent. If you establish a boundary or make a request assertively, it’s crucial to follow through and maintain that stance. Inconsistent communication can undermine your assertiveness and send mixed signals to others, making it harder to stand up for yourself in the future. For example, if you’ve assertively communicated that you are not able to take on additional work, but then later agree to do so out of guilt or pressure, you weaken your own boundary.

Being consistent with your assertiveness shows that you are serious about your needs and willing to uphold them, which encourages others to respect your limits.

Assertiveness also plays a crucial role in conflict resolution. In the workplace or personal relationships, conflicts are inevitable, but how you approach them can make all the difference. Assertive communication allows you to address conflicts head-on in a way that is solution-focused and respectful. Rather than avoiding the issue or allowing resentment to build, assertive communicators bring up the problem in a constructive manner, seeking to find a resolution that works for both parties. This proactive approach not only helps resolve the immediate conflict but also strengthens the relationship by building trust and mutual respect. Conflict resolution through assertiveness can lead to healthier, more productive interactions, where both parties feel valued and understood.

Moreover, assertiveness has long-term benefits for self-esteem and personal empowerment. By consistently standing up for your needs and expressing your feelings in a respectful way, you reinforce your sense of self-worth. Assertiveness empowers you to take control of your own experiences, rather than allowing others to dictate how you should feel or behave. This sense of empowerment can have a profound impact on all areas of life, from professional success to personal fulfillment. It encourages greater confidence in your abilities and fosters healthier, more balanced relationships, where mutual respect and understanding are the norm.

Assertive communication is an essential skill for standing up for oneself respectfully in challenging situations. By using clear, direct language, maintaining calm and neutral body language, actively listening, and expressing your feelings through "I" statements, you can communicate your needs effectively without causing further conflict. Assertiveness allows you to set boundaries, resolve conflicts, and advocate for yourself in a way that is both respectful and empowering. With practice, assertive communication can transform difficult interactions into opportunities for growth, understanding, and collaboration, ultimately leading to more positive and productive relationships.

AVOIDING DEFENSIVE RESPONSES

Avoiding defensive responses in challenging situations can be one of the most difficult, yet critical, skills to develop in maintaining healthy relationships and fostering a positive work environment. Whether it's a colleague's sharp remark, a supervisor's unexpected critique, or an unpleasant customer interaction, it's easy to feel under attack and immediately adopt a defensive posture. However, while defensiveness is a natural, reflexive reaction to perceived criticism or hostility, it rarely helps to resolve the situation and can often escalate the problem further. Learning how to recognize and avoid defensive responses not only improves communication but also enhances emotional resilience, self-awareness, and ultimately contributes to healthier interactions.

The first step in avoiding defensive responses is understanding what they are and why they occur. Defensiveness is a protective mechanism. When someone feels threatened—whether by a harsh comment, a perceived slight, or constructive criticism—the instinctive reaction is often to shield oneself by justifying actions, deflecting blame, or counterattacking. The aim of this reaction is to preserve one's self-image, avoid feelings of vulnerability, or regain control over a situation that feels uncomfortable. However, this need to defend oneself can easily be misinterpreted as unwillingness to engage in dialogue, refusal to accept responsibility, or even as hostility.

One common manifestation of defensiveness is the impulse to justify or explain away behavior in the face of criticism. For instance, if someone points out an error or a misstep, the immediate reaction might be to offer a detailed explanation of why the mistake happened or shift the blame to external factors. While this response might feel like a way to protect one's reputation or avoid fault, it often comes across as avoidance of accountability. Moreover, it prevents the person from truly hearing and reflecting on the feedback being offered. Instead of addressing the issue constructively, the focus shifts to self-protection, which may shut down further productive conversation and create tension between the parties involved.

Another form of defensiveness is counterattacking. When someone feels criticized, they may respond by pointing out the flaws or shortcomings of the other person, either subtly or overtly. This tactic is a way of deflecting attention from one's own perceived failings by shifting the spotlight onto someone else's. However, such responses rarely de-escalate the situation. Instead, they tend to escalate tensions and lead to further conflict. For example, if a colleague criticizes your work, and you respond by criticizing their recent project, the conversation quickly devolves into a tit-for-tat argument where neither person is addressing the real issue. This type of defensiveness prevents meaningful communication and problem-solving, fostering resentment rather than resolution.

Even subtle defensiveness can negatively impact interactions. Non-verbal cues, such as crossing arms, rolling eyes, or using a sarcastic tone, may signal defensiveness without any words being spoken. These non-verbal signals are just as powerful, if not more so, than verbal defensiveness, as they indicate a lack of openness to the feedback or conversation. In a professional setting, this can damage relationships with colleagues or supervisors, leading to perceptions of being unapproachable, unwilling to collaborate, or resistant to change. The key to avoiding these responses is recognizing that defensiveness often stems from internal emotions, such as insecurity, fear of judgment, or a desire to maintain control, rather than from a deliberate intention to be difficult.

Once you recognize defensiveness as a reaction that inhibits constructive dialogue, the next step is developing the tools to respond differently. One of the most effective strategies for avoiding defensiveness is to cultivate a mindset of curiosity rather than defensiveness in moments of conflict or criticism. When receiving feedback or encountering rudeness, instead of immediately reacting to protect oneself, shift your focus to understanding the other person's perspective. Ask yourself, "Why is this person saying this?" or "What can I learn from this interaction?" By reframing the situation as an opportunity for learning and growth, you create mental space to listen and respond more thoughtfully.

Active listening plays a critical role in avoiding defensive responses. When we feel attacked, the natural tendency is to interrupt, defend, or dismiss the other person's words. However, this prevents us from fully understanding the message being communicated. To avoid this, practice active listening by focusing on the speaker's words without planning your response while they're talking. Pay attention to their tone, body language, and the emotions behind their words. This not only helps you process their message more clearly but also shows that you are open to hearing their perspective. Responding with validation, such as "I hear what you're saying" or "I understand that this situation is frustrating," helps to de-escalate tension and shows that you are engaged in the conversation without reacting defensively.

Taking a moment to pause before responding can also help manage defensiveness. When confronted with criticism or rudeness, the immediate emotional reaction may be strong, leading to impulsive or defensive comments. However, taking a brief pause—whether by literally counting to five or by taking a deep breath—can provide a moment of reflection before responding. This pause allows time to consider the best response rather than reacting emotionally. By giving yourself a moment to process, you can approach the situation with a calmer, more rational mindset, which helps prevent defensive outbursts or knee-jerk reactions.

Another effective method to avoid defensiveness is to practice accepting feedback with grace, even when it is difficult to hear. No one enjoys receiving criticism, especially when it feels unfair or poorly delivered. However, recognizing that feedback—whether constructive or not—provides an opportunity for growth can help reduce the instinct to become defensive. One approach is to thank the person for their input, even if you disagree with their perspective. For example, saying, "I appreciate your feedback," followed by a calm and measured response, shows that you are receptive and willing to engage in dialogue. This approach can disarm the other person, reduce tension, and create a more constructive conversation.

Developing emotional intelligence is another crucial aspect of avoiding defensive reactions. Emotional intelligence involves being aware of your own emotions and the emotions of others, as well as managing those emotions effectively in social interactions. By improving emotional intelligence, you can better understand the triggers that lead to defensiveness and develop healthier ways to respond. For instance, if you know that you tend to feel defensive when your work is critiqued, you can prepare yourself by acknowledging this trigger and intentionally adopting a more open mindset when feedback is given. Emotional intelligence also helps in recognizing when the other person is coming from a place of stress, frustration, or insecurity, allowing you to respond with empathy rather than defensiveness.

Another key to avoiding defensiveness is to separate the content of the criticism from the delivery. Sometimes, feedback is delivered poorly or in a rude manner, but that doesn't necessarily mean the message itself lacks value. Rather than focusing on the tone or delivery, try to focus on the underlying point being made. Is there a legitimate concern being raised, even if the way it was communicated was harsh? By focusing on the substance of the message, you can avoid reacting to the tone and instead engage in a more productive conversation. This approach allows you to address the real issue without letting the manner of delivery trigger a defensive response.

Maintaining a calm, neutral tone and body language during difficult conversations is essential for avoiding defensiveness. Even when emotions are running high, consciously keeping your tone steady, your body relaxed, and your facial expressions neutral can help de-escalate the situation. This non-verbal communication signals to the other person that you are open to discussion and not reacting out of defensiveness. By maintaining control over your physical responses, you project confidence and openness, even in the face of criticism or rudeness.

It is also important to acknowledge when defensiveness has already occurred. No one is perfect, and despite the best efforts to remain calm and composed, there will be times when defensiveness slips through. In these cases, it's valuable to recognize it and take responsibility for it. If you realize that you responded defensively in a conversation, addressing it openly can help repair the interaction. A simple acknowledgment, such as "I realize I got defensive earlier, and I'd like to better understand your point," can reset the tone of the conversation and pave the way for a more productive exchange. By owning your defensiveness, you demonstrate self-awareness and a willingness to engage in honest communication, which can help rebuild trust and rapport.

Additionally, avoiding defensive responses often involves setting healthy boundaries. There is a difference between avoiding defensiveness and allowing yourself to be walked over. It is important to stand up for yourself in situations where criticism is unjust or when someone is being rude or inappropriate. However, setting boundaries can be done assertively without reacting defensively. For example, if a colleague consistently makes disrespectful comments, you might say, “I find those remarks unhelpful, and I’d prefer if we could keep our communication professional.” This sets a clear boundary without resorting to a defensive or aggressive response.

Avoiding defensive responses requires self-awareness, emotional regulation, and a commitment to constructive communication. By practicing active listening, maintaining calm body language, reframing feedback as an opportunity for growth, and acknowledging your own triggers, you can navigate difficult conversations without falling into the trap of defensiveness. This approach fosters healthier interactions, promotes problem-solving, and enhances both personal and professional relationships. While avoiding defensiveness is not always easy, especially in the face of rudeness or criticism, it is a skill that can be cultivated over time with practice and reflection. Ultimately, developing this skill leads to more productive, respectful, and empowering conversations, even in the most challenging situations.

CHAPTER 4

HUMOR AS A DEFUSING TOOL

USING HUMOR TO LIGHTEN THE MOOD

Using humor to lighten the mood in tense or awkward situations is a powerful tool that can transform interactions and foster a more positive environment, particularly in the workplace. While humor can be subjective, when applied thoughtfully and sensitively, it can ease discomfort, defuse conflict, and create connections among colleagues. The ability to introduce humor appropriately can not only help navigate difficult conversations but also enhance relationships, improve morale, and promote a culture of collaboration.

One of the key advantages of using humor in challenging interactions is its ability to disarm tension. When a conversation becomes heated or uncomfortable, introducing a light-hearted remark or a playful comment can shift the atmosphere significantly. For instance, if a colleague makes a rude comment during a meeting, a well-timed, humorous response can help everyone relax, allowing the group to move past the awkwardness. Humor can diffuse the emotional intensity of the moment, making it easier for everyone involved to regain composure and refocus on the discussion at hand. This lightening of the mood can create an environment where individuals feel more at ease expressing themselves without the fear of confrontation or escalation.

However, it's essential to understand that humor must be used judiciously. Not all situations warrant a humorous response, and poorly timed or inappropriate jokes can backfire, potentially exacerbating tension or offending others. The key to successful humor lies in its timing and relevance. An effective humorous remark should arise naturally from the context of the conversation and be tailored to the personalities and sensitivities of those involved. The aim should always be to uplift the conversation rather than trivialize serious issues or dismiss others' feelings. A successful humorous remark can reflect an understanding of the situation, showing empathy while also providing relief.

Self-deprecating humor is one effective way to employ humor without targeting others. This form of humor involves making light of one's own mistakes or quirks, and it can create an atmosphere of relatability and camaraderie. For example, if you've made an error in a presentation, acknowledging it with a light-hearted comment such as, "Well, that's one way to keep everyone awake!" can break the tension and invite laughter. By showing that you can laugh at yourself, you open the door for others to share in the moment, creating a shared experience that diminishes the awkwardness. Self-deprecating humor can also convey humility and a willingness to acknowledge imperfections, which fosters a sense of belonging and teamwork among colleagues.

Another effective approach to using humor is to employ observational humor. This type of humor highlights shared experiences or common frustrations that others can relate to, creating a sense of community. For example, if your team is navigating a particularly chaotic week, a light comment such as, "At this rate, I might need a GPS just to find my desk!" can elicit chuckles and help others realize they are not alone in their struggles. Observational humor resonates because it taps into the collective experiences of the group, reinforcing bonds and reminding everyone that they are in this together. When used thoughtfully, it can create a shared moment of levity that shifts the focus from tension to solidarity.

Situational humor can also be beneficial in the workplace. This form of humor arises from the immediate context and may include playful comments about the environment, work tasks, or ongoing projects. For instancc, if there's an ongoing office joke about the coffee machine always being out of order, you might quip, "I think our coffee machine is starting a rebellion!" Such remarks can lighten the atmosphere and foster a sense of belonging among team members, as they recognize and appreciate the shared humor in everyday frustrations. The key here is to ensure that the humor does not come at the expense of others and remains inclusive and good-natured.

In addition to easing tensions, humor can also enhance communication. When used effectively, humor can capture attention, encourage openness, and create an engaging dialogue. For instance, during team meetings, incorporating humor can stimulate discussions and make participants more willing to share their thoughts. A light-hearted comment or a funny anecdote can break the ice, making others feel more comfortable contributing to the conversation. When humor is woven into discussions, it fosters an environment where individuals feel more at ease expressing their ideas, leading to more fruitful conversations.

While humor can be a valuable tool, it's crucial to be mindful of the different senses of humor among individuals. People come from various backgrounds and cultures, which influence their understanding and appreciation of humor. What one person finds amusing, another might find offensive or unfunny. As such, it's essential to observe the reactions of others and be adaptable in your approach. Gauge the audience and their responses, adjusting your use of humor accordingly. If you notice a joke falls flat, it's wise to pivot and steer the conversation in a different direction rather than doubling down on the humor. Sensitivity to the dynamics of the group will help you use humor more effectively and ensure that it is well-received.

It's also important to recognize the boundaries when it comes to humor. Humor should never be used to belittle, ridicule, or insult others. Jokes at someone else's expense can foster animosity and create divisions among team members. Rather than bringing people together, this type of humor can create an environment of hostility, making individuals feel isolated or targeted. To cultivate a healthy workplace culture, it's essential to practice humor that is inclusive, supportive, and uplifting. Focusing on humor that celebrates shared experiences rather than drawing attention to individual shortcomings can help create a positive and encouraging atmosphere.

In addition to using humor in the moment, it's also helpful to develop a sense of humor over time. This involves cultivating an overall mindset that embraces light-heartedness and perspective, allowing for greater resilience in the face of challenges. A good sense of humor enables individuals to take themselves less seriously, which can be particularly beneficial in high-stress environments. When individuals can laugh off small inconveniences or missteps, it promotes a healthier perspective on work and encourages collaboration and support among colleagues. This mindset fosters an environment where everyone feels empowered to approach challenges with creativity and openness, knowing that it's okay to laugh through the tough times.

Moreover, humor can serve as a valuable coping mechanism. In stressful workplaces, where deadlines loom and workloads are heavy, humor can help relieve anxiety and provide a break from tension. Sharing a laugh or a funny story with colleagues can create a moment of respite, allowing everyone to recharge and refocus. It's a reminder that work, while important, does not have to be devoid of enjoyment. This balance of professionalism and playfulness can enhance overall job satisfaction and contribute to a healthier work-life balance.

While humor is a versatile tool for improving workplace dynamics, it's essential to approach it with authenticity. Authentic humor is genuine and comes from a place of sincerity. When humor is forced or feels insincere, it can have the opposite effect, creating discomfort rather than connection. Colleagues can sense inauthenticity, which can lead to distrust and disengagement. It's essential to be true to yourself and use humor that aligns with your personality and communication style. When humor comes naturally, it fosters a more relaxed atmosphere and encourages others to join in, creating a culture of openness and camaraderie.

It's also important to recognize that humor may not always be the best solution for every situation. While it can be an effective way to lighten the mood, there are moments when serious issues require serious conversations. Knowing when to use humor and when to engage more seriously is crucial for maintaining professional integrity. In instances where sensitive topics arise—such as personal struggles, conflicts, or performance issues—humor may not be appropriate and could undermine the importance of the conversation. Being attuned to the emotional landscape of the discussion helps determine when humor can be beneficial and when it may be better to adopt a more serious tone.

Ultimately, using humor to lighten the mood in challenging situations is a skill that can enhance communication, strengthen relationships, and contribute to a positive workplace culture. When employed thoughtfully and with sensitivity, humor has the power to diffuse tension, foster connections, and create a sense of belonging among team members. It allows individuals to navigate difficult conversations with grace while maintaining their integrity and professionalism. By understanding the dynamics of humor, cultivating self-awareness, and approaching situations with authenticity, individuals can embrace humor as a valuable tool in their communication toolkit. In doing so, they not only enrich their own experiences but also create an environment where everyone feels valued, connected, and empowered to contribute their best selves to the team.

WHEN HUMOR IS APPROPRIATE AND WHEN IT'S NOT

Understanding when humor is appropriate and when it is not is a crucial skill in navigating social interactions, especially in the workplace. Humor can serve as a powerful tool for diffusing tension, fostering relationships, and creating a positive atmosphere. However, it can also lead to misunderstandings, conflict, and hurt feelings if misapplied. Recognizing the nuances of humor in various contexts is essential for effective communication and maintaining professionalism.

The appropriateness of humor often depends on several factors, including the setting, the relationship between the individuals involved, the nature of the interaction, and the cultural context. In general, humor is more likely to be well-received in informal settings, where colleagues have established rapport and trust. For instance, during casual team lunches or after-work gatherings, humor can break the ice and help individuals feel more connected. In these relaxed environments, light-hearted jokes or anecdotes can create a sense of camaraderie, easing tensions and fostering a more collaborative atmosphere.

Conversely, humor may be less appropriate in formal or serious settings. Meetings that address sensitive topics, such as performance reviews, conflict resolution, or workplace issues, require a degree of professionalism and respect. In such situations, introducing humor can undermine the seriousness of the conversation and may be perceived as dismissive of the concerns at hand. When addressing sensitive matters, it is crucial to maintain an atmosphere of respect and gravity, as humor can easily be misinterpreted or come off as insincere. Therefore, it’s essential to gauge the appropriateness of humor based on the context and the emotions involved.

Understanding the dynamics of the relationship between individuals also plays a significant role in determining when humor is appropriate. If colleagues have a long-standing friendship and share a mutual understanding of each other's personalities, humor can be a natural part of their interactions. In such cases, inside jokes or light teasing can strengthen bonds and enhance workplace morale. However, if the relationship is new or if one party is in a position of authority, humor can be more complicated. Using humor in hierarchical relationships requires caution, as it may be perceived as undermining authority or not taking the situation seriously.

Cultural differences also influence perceptions of humor. What is considered funny in one culture may be viewed as offensive or inappropriate in another. Humor often relies on shared cultural references, language nuances, and social norms, making it essential to be sensitive to these differences in a diverse workplace. For instance, jokes that reference specific cultural traditions or stereotypes may not resonate with everyone and could lead to discomfort or misunderstanding. It is crucial to be aware of the backgrounds of those involved and to choose humor that is inclusive and relatable to all.

Timing is another critical factor when determining whether humor is appropriate. The moment at which humor is introduced can significantly impact how it is received. If a conversation is charged with emotion or tension, attempting to introduce humor too soon may be perceived as dismissive or trivializing the situation. In such instances, allowing individuals to express their feelings and concerns before introducing humor is advisable. Once the initial tension has subsided, humor can then serve to lighten the mood and create a more relaxed atmosphere.

On the flip side, humor can be incredibly effective in situations where the stakes are high but the tension is palpable. For example, if a team is facing a tight deadline and stress levels are rising, a well-timed humorous remark can provide a much-needed release. In these moments, humor can serve as a coping mechanism, helping individuals navigate the challenges they face. Recognizing the right moment to introduce humor requires a keen sense of observation and empathy toward the emotional climate of the room.

While humor can foster connection and camaraderie, it is essential to remember that humor should never come at the expense of others. Jokes that target individuals or groups, particularly those based on personal attributes such as appearance, ethnicity, gender, or beliefs, can be harmful and create an environment of hostility. Such humor is rarely appropriate and can lead to significant consequences, including damaged relationships and decreased morale. It is vital to be aware of the potential impact of one's words and to choose humor that uplifts rather than belittles.

The intention behind humor also matters significantly. When humor is rooted in kindness and genuine intent, it is more likely to be well-received. For example, making a playful remark about a shared experience, such as the challenges of navigating office technology, can create a sense of solidarity and connection. In contrast, sarcasm or humor that appears mocking can lead to misunderstandings and hurt feelings. It is essential to ensure that humor aligns with the values of respect and empathy, as this will contribute to a positive workplace culture.

Moreover, understanding the audience is critical in determining the appropriateness of humor. Different individuals have varying thresholds for humor, and what might be funny to one person could be uncomfortable for another. When interacting with colleagues, it is essential to observe their reactions and gauge their comfort levels. If individuals appear disengaged, uncomfortable, or offended, it is a sign that humor may not be resonating well in that context. Being attuned to the reactions of others allows individuals to navigate social interactions more effectively and adjust their communication style accordingly.

Another key consideration is the context of the conversation. Humor can often be used as a transition between topics or to ease into a more serious discussion. For instance, if a team is preparing to discuss a challenging project outcome, a light-hearted remark about the learning experience can set the tone for a constructive dialogue. By framing the conversation with humor, individuals can create an environment where colleagues feel more comfortable sharing their thoughts and ideas. However, the humor must remain relevant to the topic at hand, as straying too far can lead to confusion and disengagement.

Furthermore, the medium of communication also plays a role in the appropriateness of humor. In face-to-face interactions, individuals can rely on non-verbal cues and body language to gauge reactions and adjust their humor accordingly. However, in written communications such as emails or messages, the nuances of humor can be easily lost. What may come across as a light-hearted comment in person could be misinterpreted in writing, leading to potential misunderstandings. In written formats, it is often best to err on the side of caution and avoid humor unless the context clearly supports it.

When navigating humor in professional settings, it is also vital to be prepared for varying responses. While humor can be a great icebreaker, it may not always elicit laughter or agreement. Some individuals may prefer to maintain a more serious demeanor, while others may embrace humor wholeheartedly. Being receptive to these differences and adjusting one's approach can help maintain positive interactions. If humor falls flat, gracefully acknowledging it and shifting back to the matter at hand demonstrates professionalism and self-awareness.

Moreover, it's essential to cultivate a culture where humor is welcomed but not forced. Encouraging a workplace culture that values positivity and camaraderie can create an environment where humor flourishes naturally. When humor is embraced as a part of the workplace culture, individuals feel more comfortable expressing themselves and connecting with one another. Leaders and managers can set the tone by modeling appropriate humor, showing how it can enhance collaboration and relationships while respecting boundaries.

Lastly, recognizing that humor has its limitations is essential. While it can be a powerful tool for enhancing communication and fostering relationships, there are times when serious conversations must take precedence. Addressing performance issues, providing constructive feedback, or discussing personal matters may require a more straightforward approach. In such cases, prioritizing respect and understanding over humor ensures that individuals feel heard and valued.

The appropriateness of humor hinges on context, relationships, cultural sensitivities, timing, and intention. Navigating humor effectively in professional settings requires a keen awareness of these factors to ensure that humor enhances interactions rather than detracts from them. When used thoughtfully, humor can be a valuable tool for creating positive workplace dynamics, fostering connections, and lightening the mood. By understanding when to employ humor and when to adopt a more serious tone, individuals can navigate social interactions with confidence and grace, contributing to a healthier and more productive work environment.

CHAPTER 5

SETTING BOUNDARIES

IDENTIFYING UNACCEPTABLE BEHAVIOR

Identifying unacceptable behavior in the workplace is crucial for fostering a respectful and productive environment. Unacceptable behavior can take many forms, ranging from overt hostility to subtle undermining tactics. Understanding these behaviors is essential not only for individuals who may be on the receiving end but also for organizations striving to create a culture of professionalism and respect. By recognizing unacceptable behavior, individuals can address issues before they escalate and contribute to a healthier workplace atmosphere.

At the core of unacceptable behavior is the violation of workplace norms and the disregard for the dignity of others. Such behaviors can manifest in various ways, including verbal abuse, inappropriate comments, bullying, harassment, and passive-aggressive actions. Identifying these behaviors is the first step in addressing them effectively.

Verbal abuse is one of the most overt forms of unacceptable behavior. It includes yelling, swearing, or using derogatory language toward another person. Verbal abuse not only creates a hostile environment but can also lead to significant emotional distress for the recipient. Such behavior often stems from frustration or stress but becomes unacceptable when it is directed at others. For instance, a manager who raises their voice during a meeting in response to a perceived mistake may intimidate employees, discouraging them from voicing their opinions or concerns. Recognizing the impact of verbal abuse is essential for fostering a culture of open communication and respect.

Inappropriate comments are another manifestation of unacceptable behavior. These can range from offensive jokes to remarks about someone's appearance or personal life. While humor can sometimes lighten the mood, it can also cross boundaries and make individuals feel uncomfortable. Comments that objectify, stereotype, or belittle others, particularly based on gender, race, or sexual orientation, are unacceptable. It is essential to understand that what may be deemed as harmless banter by one person can be deeply hurtful to another. Being aware of the language used in conversations and ensuring that it remains respectful and inclusive is vital in identifying unacceptable behavior.

Bullying is a pervasive issue in many workplaces, characterized by repeated aggressive behavior intended to intimidate or harm an individual. This can include spreading rumors, isolating someone from their peers, or undermining their work. Unlike one-off incidents, bullying is systematic and can have devastating effects on the mental health of those targeted. Bullying can create a toxic work environment, leading to decreased morale, productivity, and overall job satisfaction. Recognizing the signs of bullying, such as changes in an individual's behavior, increased absenteeism, or visible distress, is crucial for addressing the issue effectively.

Harassment, whether sexual or otherwise, represents another severe form of unacceptable behavior. Sexual harassment can encompass a wide range of actions, from unwanted advances and inappropriate touching to suggestive comments or sharing explicit materials. Such behavior creates a hostile environment that not only affects the victim but can also impact the morale and productivity of the entire team. It is essential to understand that harassment is not just about intent; it is also about the perception of the recipient. An individual may feel harassed regardless of whether the perpetrator intended to be offensive. Establishing clear policies regarding harassment and ensuring that all employees are educated on these policies is essential for creating a safe workplace.

Passive-aggressive behavior is often more challenging to identify because it may not be overtly confrontational. Instead, it involves indirect expressions of hostility, such as sarcasm, procrastination, or intentional inefficiency. For example, an employee who fails to complete a task on time as a way to express dissatisfaction or resentment is engaging in passive-aggressive behavior. This type of behavior can create confusion and tension in the workplace, making it difficult for teams to function cohesively. Being attuned to the subtleties of passive-aggressive behavior and addressing it promptly can prevent the escalation of conflicts and foster a more transparent environment.

Another critical aspect of identifying unacceptable behavior is recognizing the context in which it occurs. Certain behaviors may be deemed acceptable in informal settings but are inappropriate in professional environments. For instance, a joking comment among friends may not translate well into a workplace setting, especially if it touches on sensitive subjects. Understanding the nuances of workplace dynamics and the expectations for professional conduct can help individuals navigate social interactions more effectively.

It is also important to acknowledge that unacceptable behavior can stem from various underlying factors, such as stress, frustration, or personal issues. Individuals experiencing high levels of stress may be more prone to lash out or exhibit uncharacteristic behavior. However, while understanding the context of unacceptable behavior can foster empathy, it does not excuse it. It is essential to address the behavior directly, regardless of the underlying causes. Encouraging open communication and providing support for those facing challenges can help mitigate the occurrence of unacceptable behavior.

Identifying unacceptable behavior also involves recognizing patterns. One-off incidents may not warrant significant concern, but when certain behaviors become recurring themes, it is crucial to address them. Patterns of negative behavior can lead to a toxic work environment that diminishes morale and productivity. For example, if an employee consistently interrupts their colleagues during meetings or frequently dismisses their ideas, these behaviors must be addressed before they become entrenched.

Another important consideration is the role of leadership in modeling acceptable behavior. Leaders set the tone for workplace culture, and their actions significantly influence the behavior of their teams. If leaders engage in or tolerate unacceptable behavior, it sends a message that such conduct is permissible. Conversely, when leaders model respect, open communication, and accountability, it encourages others to do the same. Encouraging leadership to actively participate in training on acceptable workplace behavior and to promote a culture of respect can have a significant positive impact.

Training and education play a vital role in identifying and addressing unacceptable behavior. Organizations can implement programs to educate employees about workplace etiquette, diversity and inclusion, and the importance of respectful communication. Providing resources and support for individuals who may experience or witness unacceptable behavior is equally important. Establishing clear reporting mechanisms and creating safe spaces for individuals to voice their concerns can help address issues before they escalate.

Moreover, it is essential to create an environment where individuals feel empowered to speak up about unacceptable behavior. Fear of retaliation or dismissal can prevent employees from reporting inappropriate conduct, leading to a culture of silence. Organizations must emphasize the importance of addressing unacceptable behavior and reassure employees that their concerns will be taken seriously. Fostering a culture of transparency and accountability encourages individuals to engage in constructive conversations about behavior that needs to change.

In addition to identifying unacceptable behavior, it is important to recognize the signs that indicate it is time to intervene. If certain behaviors persist despite discussions or attempts to address them, it may be necessary to escalate the issue. Indicators of persistent unacceptable behavior may include continued complaints from multiple employees, noticeable declines in team morale or productivity, and an increase in interpersonal conflicts. When these signs are present, it is crucial to take proactive measures to address the underlying issues.

One effective approach to addressing unacceptable behavior is through constructive feedback. Providing feedback involves discussing the specific behaviors that are problematic and outlining their impact on the workplace. It is essential to approach these conversations with empathy and a focus on improvement rather than blame. Encouraging open dialogue allows individuals to express their perspectives and fosters a collaborative approach to finding solutions.

Furthermore, conflict resolution strategies can play a vital role in addressing unacceptable behavior. Implementing techniques such as mediation, where a neutral third party facilitates discussions between conflicting individuals, can help individuals find common ground and resolve their differences. Providing training on conflict resolution skills equips employees with the tools they need to navigate challenging situations effectively.

Ultimately, identifying unacceptable behavior requires vigilance, empathy, and a commitment to fostering a respectful workplace culture. It involves recognizing overt actions, subtle dynamics, and the broader context in which they occur. By understanding and addressing unacceptable behavior, individuals and organizations can create an environment where everyone feels valued, respected, and empowered to contribute their best work. As workplaces continue to evolve, embracing a culture of respect and accountability will be essential for building strong teams and ensuring long-term success.

CLEARLY COMMUNICATING BOUNDARIES

In today's fast-paced and often high-pressure workplace environments, clearly communicating boundaries has never been more crucial. Boundaries are the invisible lines that define acceptable behavior and set limits on what is permissible in interactions with colleagues. They are essential not only for maintaining personal well-being but also for fostering a productive and respectful workplace culture. The challenge often lies in articulating these boundaries effectively, especially when confronted with rudeness or inappropriate behavior.

Understanding what boundaries are and why they matter is the first step in establishing them. Boundaries can be physical, emotional, or psychological. Physical boundaries pertain to personal space and comfort levels regarding proximity to others. Emotional boundaries involve how much of one's emotional self one is willing to share and how one reacts to the emotions of others. Psychological boundaries encompass one's mental well-being and the ability to maintain personal beliefs and values despite external pressures. Each type of boundary plays a critical role in maintaining a healthy workplace atmosphere, where individuals can perform their best work without feeling threatened or undervalued.

Communicating boundaries starts with self-awareness. It requires an understanding of one's limits and the recognition of situations where those limits are being tested. Reflecting on past interactions can provide valuable insights. For instance, consider moments when someone's comments made you feel uncomfortable or when a colleague's behavior intruded on your ability to concentrate. Recognizing these instances helps clarify what specific boundaries need to be established or reinforced.

Once an individual has identified their boundaries, the next step is to communicate them clearly and assertively. This process can be daunting, especially in a workplace setting where power dynamics and relationships can complicate direct communication. However, it is essential to remember that setting boundaries is not an act of aggression; rather, it is a form of self-care and a means of fostering mutual respect. Effective boundary communication is characterized by clarity, firmness, and respect. It is vital to use "I" statements that express feelings and needs without blaming or attacking the other person. For example, instead of saying, "You always interrupt me," one might say, "I feel undervalued when I am interrupted during meetings. I'd appreciate it if we could allow each person to finish their thoughts before responding." This approach emphasizes the speaker's feelings while reducing the likelihood of defensiveness from the other party.

Timing also plays a crucial role in boundary setting. It is best to communicate boundaries when emotions are stable and the environment is conducive to a calm discussion. Engaging in boundary discussions during heightened emotional states, such as after a conflict or during a stressful moment, can lead to misunderstandings and escalation. Choosing a neutral time, perhaps during a regular check-in or team meeting, can create a more conducive atmosphere for addressing boundaries.

In addition to verbal communication, non-verbal cues significantly impact how boundaries are perceived. Body language, tone of voice, and eye contact all contribute to the effectiveness of boundary-setting conversations. Maintaining an open posture, steady eye contact, and a calm tone can convey confidence and seriousness, underscoring the importance of the boundaries being set. Conversely, closed-off body language or a hesitant tone can lead others to dismiss or misinterpret the communicated boundaries.

Moreover, it is essential to anticipate potential reactions when communicating boundaries. People may respond in various ways, ranging from acceptance to defensiveness or even hostility. Understanding that others may need time to process the boundaries being communicated can help manage expectations. It is also crucial to stand firm in one's boundaries, regardless of how others react. This firmness does not equate to being inflexible; rather, it reflects a commitment to one's well-being and respect for oneself.

In some cases, individuals may struggle with asserting boundaries due to fear of conflict or concerns about how their colleagues will perceive them. It is important to recognize that failing to establish boundaries can lead to increased stress, burnout, and resentment. It can also perpetuate a culture of disrespect where rudeness becomes normalized. Therefore, cultivating the courage to communicate boundaries effectively is an investment in one's own mental health and the overall work environment.

Boundaries are not merely limitations; they also serve as guidelines for healthy interactions. By clearly communicating what is acceptable, individuals can help set the tone for professional relationships. For example, if a colleague tends to dominate conversations and consistently interrupts others, addressing this behavior by expressing the desire for a more equitable dialogue can help shift the dynamic. Communicating boundaries can encourage others to reflect on their behavior and contribute to a culture of mutual respect and collaboration.

Additionally, revisiting and reinforcing boundaries is a necessary part of the process. Just as boundaries may evolve over time due to changes in personal circumstances or workplace dynamics, it is vital to revisit them periodically. This may involve having check-in conversations with colleagues to ensure everyone is on the same page and to address any emerging issues. Open communication fosters trust and encourages a supportive workplace culture where boundaries can be respected and reinforced.

Another significant aspect of clearly communicating boundaries involves understanding the organizational culture and the existing dynamics within a team. Every workplace has its norms regarding communication and interaction, and navigating these dynamics requires tact and consideration. Understanding how to align personal boundaries with the collective culture can facilitate smoother interactions. For example, in a highly collaborative environment, individuals may need to balance their boundaries with the need for teamwork. This balance can be achieved by expressing boundaries in a manner that emphasizes collaboration, such as stating, “I value our teamwork and want to ensure we can all contribute our ideas without interruption.”

Conflict resolution skills are also beneficial when communicating boundaries. Should a boundary be crossed, having strategies in place to address the situation constructively is crucial. Instead of allowing resentment to build, addressing the issue promptly can prevent it from escalating into a more significant problem. Utilizing “I” statements and focusing on specific behaviors rather than personal attacks can help de-escalate tensions and facilitate constructive dialogue.

Furthermore, it is essential to recognize that communicating boundaries is an ongoing process that requires continuous effort. As individuals develop their assertiveness and confidence, they may encounter new challenges that necessitate further boundary-setting discussions. Embracing this process as a growth opportunity can alleviate some of the pressure associated with boundary communication. Each successful interaction can serve as a learning experience, equipping individuals with the skills and confidence to navigate future challenges.

In the context of addressing rudeness, clearly communicating boundaries becomes even more significant.

Rudeness can often stem from a lack of awareness regarding acceptable behavior. By addressing rudeness directly and asserting personal boundaries, individuals can provide an opportunity for the offending party to reflect on their behavior. This not only promotes accountability but also encourages a culture of open dialogue where individuals feel empowered to express their discomfort.

Moreover, the impact of clearly communicated boundaries extends beyond individual interactions. When employees model respectful behavior and assertiveness, it can create a ripple effect throughout the organization. Colleagues may feel inspired to set their own boundaries, contributing to a culture that prioritizes respect and professionalism. Conversely, when boundaries are not communicated effectively, the organization may risk cultivating an environment where disrespect and rudeness are tolerated.

Additionally, organizations can support boundary-setting efforts by fostering a culture of open communication and providing training on effective communication skills. Workshops and seminars can equip employees with the tools they need to articulate their boundaries and navigate challenging interactions. By prioritizing communication and respect at the organizational level, companies can create an environment where boundaries are valued and upheld.

Clearly communicating boundaries is an essential aspect of maintaining a respectful and productive workplace. It requires self-awareness, assertiveness, and a commitment to fostering a culture of respect. By articulating boundaries effectively, individuals can protect their well-being, promote healthy interactions, and contribute to a positive work environment. As employees grow in their ability to communicate boundaries, they will not only enhance their personal experiences but also help cultivate a workplace culture that values respect, collaboration, and professionalism.

CONSEQUENCES OF CROSSING BOUNDARIES

In any workplace, boundaries serve as essential guidelines that define acceptable behavior and maintain a respectful environment. When these boundaries are crossed, the consequences can be far-reaching, affecting not only the individuals involved but also the overall dynamics of the workplace. Understanding the potential repercussions of crossing boundaries is crucial for cultivating a healthy, productive work environment where everyone feels safe, valued, and empowered to perform at their best.

At its core, crossing boundaries disrupts the delicate balance of interpersonal relationships. When someone disregards another person's boundaries, it can lead to feelings of discomfort, resentment, and violation. For the individual whose boundaries have been crossed, the immediate emotional toll can be significant. They may experience anger, frustration, or anxiety, all of which can detract from their focus and productivity. The emotional fallout from boundary violations can lead to a decline in job satisfaction and motivation, creating a toxic atmosphere that stifles creativity and collaboration.

Moreover, when boundaries are crossed repeatedly, the impact can extend beyond the immediate relationship. Trust is a fundamental component of effective teamwork and collaboration. Once trust is eroded due to boundary violations, it can take a long time to rebuild. Colleagues may become hesitant to engage in open dialogue or share ideas, fearing that their contributions will not be respected. This reluctance can stifle innovation and prevent the team from fully capitalizing on its collective strengths.

The consequences of crossing boundaries can also manifest in physical and mental health issues. Stress is a common response to feelings of violation and disrespect, and chronic stress can lead to serious health problems. Employees may experience symptoms such as fatigue, headaches, and gastrointestinal issues as their bodies react to the ongoing strain. Furthermore, mental health can suffer, leading to conditions such as anxiety or depression. This can result in absenteeism or presenteeism, where employees are physically present but emotionally and mentally disengaged, further impacting overall productivity.

In the context of workplace dynamics, crossing boundaries can lead to increased conflict. When one person feels that their boundaries have been disregarded, they may react defensively or aggressively. This reaction can escalate tensions within the team, resulting in a hostile work environment. Conflicts can quickly spiral out of control, leading to confrontations that not only disrupt workflow but can also create lasting divides among colleagues. The emotional climate of the workplace can suffer, leading to a pervasive atmosphere of distrust and dissatisfaction.

Additionally, crossing boundaries may have repercussions on a more formal level, such as disciplinary action or even termination. Many organizations have policies in place to address harassment, bullying, or other inappropriate behavior. When someone crosses established boundaries, they may be subject to these policies, which can include warnings, reprimands, or other consequences. For organizations, failing to address boundary violations can lead to liability issues, especially if a pattern of behavior is allowed to persist. This could result in legal consequences for the organization, along with reputational damage that affects employee morale and recruitment efforts.

Boundary violations can also hinder professional development. Individuals who experience repeated violations may become less inclined to pursue growth opportunities, fearing that their contributions will not be respected or valued. They may withdraw from collaborative projects or refrain from sharing innovative ideas, which can stifle their career progression. Moreover, the fear of crossing boundaries themselves can lead to a culture of silence where individuals do not voice concerns or feedback, perpetuating a cycle of disengagement.

Communication breakdowns often accompany the crossing of boundaries. When individuals do not feel safe expressing their needs or concerns, misunderstandings can proliferate. Communication is the backbone of effective teamwork, and when it falters, the entire team can suffer. Tasks may become misaligned, and goals may be obscured, resulting in wasted time and resources. Effective communication relies on mutual respect and trust, both of which can be severely undermined by boundary violations.

The impact of crossing boundaries is not limited to the immediate work environment; it can also have implications for an organization's culture. A workplace that tolerates boundary violations can inadvertently signal to employees that such behavior is acceptable. This can lead to a culture where rudeness or disrespect becomes normalized, creating a vicious cycle that is difficult to break. In contrast, organizations that prioritize boundary-setting and respect tend to foster an environment where employees feel valued and empowered. This positive culture not only enhances employee satisfaction but also improves retention rates and overall performance.

In the broader context of leadership, crossing boundaries can hinder effective management. Leaders play a pivotal role in setting the tone for workplace culture. When leaders disregard boundaries, either through their actions or inaction, they model unacceptable behavior for their teams. This can lead to a cascade effect, where team members feel empowered to mimic such behavior, perpetuating a cycle of disrespect. Conversely, leaders who model respect for boundaries and encourage open communication can foster a culture of accountability and collaboration.

For individuals who consistently cross boundaries, the consequences can be career-altering. Over time, repeated violations can lead to a damaged reputation within the organization. Colleagues may begin to view them as unprofessional or unreliable, which can hinder their career advancement. Moreover, individuals who fail to recognize the impact of their behavior on others may find themselves isolated within the workplace, as colleagues distance themselves from someone who does not respect their boundaries. This isolation can exacerbate feelings of frustration and defensiveness, further entrenching the individual in negative patterns of behavior.

In the context of diversity and inclusion, crossing boundaries can also have significant implications. Workplaces are increasingly diverse, with individuals from various backgrounds, cultures, and experiences. Each individual brings unique perspectives and boundaries that reflect their identity and experiences. Failing to respect these diverse boundaries can lead to misunderstandings and feelings of exclusion. This not only harms individual employees but can also prevent organizations from fully benefiting from the richness of diverse viewpoints. A culture that embraces and respects boundaries fosters inclusion, allowing all employees to contribute authentically to the organization's mission.

Additionally, the consequences of crossing boundaries can extend to employee recruitment and retention. Potential hires often assess an organization's culture and values during the interview process. A workplace that is known for boundary violations or disrespect may struggle to attract top talent. In contrast, organizations that prioritize respect and communication tend to draw candidates who value collaboration and professionalism. Moreover, when employees feel disrespected or undervalued, they are more likely to seek opportunities elsewhere. High turnover rates can be costly for organizations, leading to recruitment expenses, training costs, and disruptions in productivity.

Ultimately, addressing boundary violations requires a collective commitment from all employees, from leadership to entry-level staff. Organizations must create clear policies that outline acceptable behavior and establish consequences for violations. Training programs can equip employees with the skills needed to recognize and communicate boundaries effectively. Moreover, fostering a culture of accountability and respect can empower individuals to speak up when they feel their boundaries have been crossed. This can create a safer and more inclusive workplace where everyone feels valued and respected.

The consequences of crossing boundaries in the workplace are profound and multifaceted. They affect individuals on emotional, mental, and physical levels, disrupt team dynamics, and can lead to formal repercussions for both individuals and organizations. By recognizing the importance of boundaries and fostering a culture of respect, organizations can create an environment where employees thrive. Establishing clear expectations and encouraging open communication are essential components in preventing boundary violations and their associated consequences. Ultimately, a commitment to respecting boundaries not only enhances individual well-being but also contributes to a positive, productive workplace culture where everyone can succeed.

PART III

Dealing with Difficult People

CHAPTER 6
THE BULLY

RECOGNIZING BULLYING BEHAVIOR

Recognizing bullying behavior in the workplace is essential for maintaining a healthy, productive environment. Bullying is not only detrimental to individual employees but can also undermine team cohesion and overall organizational culture. While many people may equate bullying with overt aggression, such as physical threats or blatant harassment, workplace bullying can manifest in various subtle and insidious forms. To effectively address bullying, it is crucial to understand its characteristics, dynamics, and the context in which it occurs.

At its core, bullying is characterized by a power imbalance. It typically involves an individual or a group exerting power over another person, often with the intention of causing harm, distress, or intimidation. This imbalance can be established through various means, such as hierarchical authority, social influence, or even charisma. The perpetrator may wield power consciously or unconsciously, but the impact on the victim is usually profound and lasting. This power dynamic is what differentiates bullying from ordinary conflict or disagreements, as it often involves a pattern of behavior aimed at undermining the victim's confidence, dignity, or self-worth.

One of the most common forms of bullying in the workplace is verbal abuse, which can range from belittling comments to outright insults. Verbal bullies may engage in mocking, name-calling, or harsh criticism, often targeting specific attributes of the victim. Such behavior not only inflicts emotional pain but also creates a toxic environment where fear and anxiety thrive. Victims of verbal bullying may feel isolated and marginalized, which can significantly affect their morale, performance, and willingness to engage with colleagues.

Another common form of bullying is social exclusion or isolation. This behavior involves deliberately excluding someone from social interactions or group activities, often with the intent of ostracizing them. Social bullies may spread rumors, manipulate relationships, or engage in gossip to undermine the victim's reputation. The emotional toll of social bullying can be profound, as individuals may feel lonely and unsupported, leading to a decline in mental health and overall job satisfaction. This form of bullying can be particularly damaging because it often occurs behind closed doors, making it challenging for outsiders to recognize or intervene.

In addition to verbal abuse and social exclusion, bullying can also manifest through aggressive or threatening behaviors. This includes intimidation tactics, such as aggressive body language, invading personal space, or using a loud, hostile tone. These behaviors create an atmosphere of fear and apprehension, as victims may feel physically threatened or emotionally overwhelmed. While these aggressive behaviors are often more recognizable than other forms of bullying, they can still go unnoticed in a busy workplace, particularly if colleagues prioritize productivity over interpersonal dynamics.

Bullying can also take the form of manipulation or coercion. This occurs when an individual uses their position of power to manipulate or control others, often exploiting vulnerabilities to achieve their goals. For instance, a manager might use their authority to pressure employees into compromising situations, such as working overtime without pay or engaging in unethical practices. This form of bullying is particularly insidious because it often operates under the guise of legitimate authority, making it challenging for victims to recognize and address the behavior without fear of repercussions.

Another significant aspect of recognizing bullying behavior is understanding the context in which it occurs. Workplace culture plays a vital role in shaping interpersonal dynamics and can either exacerbate or mitigate bullying behavior. In environments where competition is encouraged over collaboration, individuals may feel pressured to engage in bullying behaviors to gain an advantage. Conversely, workplaces that prioritize teamwork and open communication are less likely to foster bullying behaviors, as employees feel supported and valued.

It is essential to recognize that bullying is not solely an issue of individual behavior but can also stem from systemic issues within an organization. For instance, a culture that tolerates aggressive competition, lacks clear policies on acceptable behavior, or fails to address conflict constructively can inadvertently create an environment conducive to bullying. In such contexts, employees may feel unsupported in speaking out against bullying behavior, leading to a cycle of silence and perpetuation of harmful practices.

Moreover, recognizing bullying behavior requires an awareness of its impact on both the victim and the broader workplace environment. Victims of bullying often experience a range of negative outcomes, including increased stress, anxiety, depression, and physical health issues. These effects can lead to absenteeism, reduced productivity, and high turnover rates, which ultimately harm the organization as a whole. When bullying goes unchecked, it can create a culture of fear and distrust, leading to decreased morale and collaboration among employees.

One of the critical challenges in recognizing bullying behavior is the tendency for victims to internalize the abuse. Many individuals who experience bullying may feel ashamed, embarrassed, or powerless to confront the perpetrator. They may believe that the bullying is their fault or that they deserve the treatment they are receiving. This internalization can prevent victims from speaking out or seeking support, allowing the bullying behavior to continue unchecked. It is essential to foster an environment where employees feel safe discussing their experiences and seeking assistance without fear of retribution.

Recognizing bullying behavior also involves paying attention to the warning signs exhibited by both the victim and the perpetrator. Victims may show signs of distress, such as withdrawing from social interactions, exhibiting decreased confidence, or experiencing changes in their work performance. They may also express feelings of hopelessness or fear regarding their work environment. On the other hand, perpetrators may display patterns of aggressive or dismissive behavior, demonstrating a lack of empathy for others' feelings or well-being.

It is equally important to recognize that bullying behavior can have far-reaching consequences beyond the immediate interactions between individuals. The ripple effect of bullying can impact team dynamics, leading to decreased trust and collaboration among colleagues. Teams plagued by bullying behaviors may struggle with communication and cohesion, as employees become wary of one another and hesitant to engage in open dialogue. This breakdown in trust can lead to a lack of creativity and innovation, as individuals may be less willing to share ideas or take risks in a toxic environment.

Furthermore, the recognition of bullying behavior can contribute to a broader understanding of the importance of mental health in the workplace. Addressing bullying is not merely about preventing harmful behaviors; it is also about promoting well-being and resilience among employees. Organizations that prioritize mental health initiatives and provide support for victims of bullying can create a culture that fosters healing and growth. This proactive approach can lead to increased employee engagement and retention, as individuals feel valued and supported in their workplace.

In recognizing bullying behavior, it is essential to foster a culture of accountability and open communication. Organizations should establish clear policies that outline acceptable behavior and consequences for bullying. Training programs can equip employees with the skills needed to identify bullying behaviors and address them constructively. Encouraging bystander intervention and empowering employees to speak up when they witness bullying can create a collective responsibility for maintaining a respectful workplace.

Ultimately, recognizing bullying behavior is crucial for creating a safe and inclusive workplace. By understanding the various forms of bullying and their impact on individuals and the organization, employers and employees can work together to foster a culture of respect and support. This proactive approach not only enhances employee well-being but also contributes to a more productive and engaged workforce. By addressing bullying behavior head-on, organizations can create an environment where everyone feels valued, respected, and empowered to thrive.

STRATEGIES FOR DEALING WITH BULLIES

Dealing with bullies in the workplace requires a multifaceted approach, as their behavior can undermine not only individual well-being but also overall workplace morale and productivity. It is crucial to recognize that bullying is often rooted in a power imbalance, where the bully seeks to exert control or influence over their target. To effectively address bullying, individuals must equip themselves with strategies that empower them to respond constructively while also safeguarding their mental and emotional health.

The first step in addressing bullying behavior is to acknowledge the issue openly and honestly. Denying or minimizing the impact of bullying only allows the behavior to persist and can exacerbate feelings of isolation and helplessness in the victim. Recognizing the signs of bullying is essential; this includes understanding the verbal and non-verbal cues that indicate a hostile environment. The victim must validate their feelings and experiences, recognizing that they are legitimate and deserve attention. By affirming the reality of the situation, individuals can begin to build a foundation for effective responses.

Once the issue has been acknowledged, the next step is to gather evidence of the bullying behavior. Documenting specific incidents, including dates, times, and descriptions of what transpired, can provide a concrete record that can be invaluable when addressing the behavior with management or HR. This documentation should focus not only on the events themselves but also on their emotional impact. Victims may want to record how these incidents affected their work performance, relationships with colleagues, and overall mental health. This approach empowers individuals to present their case more convincingly and demonstrates that the behavior is not an isolated incident but rather a pattern of conduct.

Having gathered evidence, it is crucial to analyze the context in which the bullying occurs. Understanding the power dynamics at play can provide insights into why the bully behaves as they do and how to respond effectively. For instance, some bullies may operate out of insecurity, projecting their fears onto others in an attempt to feel more powerful. Recognizing these motivations can help victims disarm the bully by refusing to engage with their attempts to intimidate. Furthermore, this understanding can aid in developing responses that focus on assertiveness rather than aggression, helping to defuse the situation rather than escalate it.

In many cases, assertive communication becomes a vital tool for dealing with bullies. Unlike aggressive communication, which can provoke further hostility, assertive communication focuses on expressing one's feelings and needs without placing blame. This approach allows victims to stand up for themselves while maintaining their dignity and composure. For example, if a bully makes a derogatory comment, an assertive response might be, “I feel disrespected when you say that. I’d appreciate it if you could refrain from making such comments in the future.” This statement clearly communicates the impact of the bully’s behavior while setting a boundary for future interactions.

In addition to assertive communication, individuals may also benefit from employing a technique known as the “broken record” method. This involves calmly repeating one’s request or assertion, regardless of the bully's attempts to divert or escalate the conversation. By maintaining a consistent message, victims can reinforce their boundaries and demonstrate that they will not be swayed by manipulative tactics. For instance, if a bully tries to belittle the victim's concerns, they might respond with, “I understand that you have a different perspective, but I need to express my feelings on this matter.” This approach emphasizes the victim's agency and determination to address the situation.

Another effective strategy is to leverage the power of support networks within the workplace. Building relationships with colleagues who share similar values and attitudes can create a buffer against bullying behavior. Supportive coworkers can serve as witnesses to bullying incidents, which adds credibility to the victim’s claims. Moreover, having allies can provide emotional validation and encouragement, fostering a sense of belonging that bullies often seek to undermine. Establishing a culture of mutual support not only helps individuals feel less isolated but also promotes a healthier workplace environment overall.

When faced with persistent bullying, individuals may need to consider escalating the issue to management or human resources. This step should not be taken lightly, as it can create additional tension within the workplace. However, if the bullying behavior continues despite assertive attempts to address it, involving a higher authority may be necessary. When approaching management or HR, it is crucial to present the evidence gathered, clearly articulate the impact of the bullying on one's work and well-being, and propose potential solutions. This proactive approach demonstrates that the victim is not seeking to create conflict but rather to resolve an ongoing issue in a constructive manner.

In addition to seeking support within the workplace, individuals may also consider external resources, such as counseling or professional development programs. Speaking with a therapist can help victims process their feelings and develop coping strategies for managing the emotional toll of bullying. Engaging in professional development can also empower individuals to enhance their skills in conflict resolution, communication, and assertiveness. These tools can prove invaluable when navigating challenging workplace dynamics and can foster a greater sense of confidence in dealing with difficult situations.

In some cases, it may be necessary to confront the bully directly. However, this approach should be considered carefully, as it can lead to unpredictable outcomes. If an individual chooses to address the bully, it is essential to do so in a calm and controlled manner. Rather than approaching the situation with anger or aggression, the victim should aim to engage in a constructive dialogue. For example, they might say, "I'd like to discuss our recent interactions. I feel that some of your comments have been hurtful, and I'd appreciate it if we could communicate more respectfully moving forward." This type of confrontation can serve to illuminate the bully's behavior and prompt a change in their actions.

It is important to note that not all bullying behavior can be resolved through direct confrontation. In cases where the bully remains unresponsive or escalates their behavior, individuals may need to prioritize their well-being and consider their options. This may include seeking a transfer to another department, looking for new employment opportunities, or taking a temporary leave of absence to recover from the stress of the situation. Ultimately, the goal is to create a work environment that fosters respect, collaboration, and personal well-being, and sometimes that means making difficult choices for the sake of one's mental health.

Addressing bullying behavior also involves reflecting on the broader organizational culture and advocating for systemic change. Individuals can play a role in promoting a workplace environment that discourages bullying by participating in initiatives that emphasize respect, inclusion, and open communication. This may include supporting anti-bullying policies, participating in training sessions, or advocating for mental health resources within the organization. By contributing to a culture that prioritizes kindness and accountability, individuals can help mitigate bullying behavior not only for themselves but for their colleagues as well.

Dealing with bullies in the workplace requires a combination of self-advocacy, assertive communication, and support from colleagues. By acknowledging the behavior, documenting incidents, and employing effective strategies, individuals can take control of their situation and foster a more respectful environment. It is essential to understand that addressing bullying is not only about protecting oneself but also about promoting a culture of dignity and collaboration in the workplace. As individuals become empowered to stand up against bullying behavior, they contribute to a healthier and more productive workplace for everyone.

SEEKING SUPPORT FROM HR OR A SUPERVISOR

In any workplace, navigating interpersonal relationships can often be a challenging endeavor. While most interactions are straightforward, conflicts can arise, leading to uncomfortable situations that require tact and sensitivity. In particular, when faced with rudeness or inappropriate behavior, it can become crucial to seek support from human resources (HR) or a supervisor. This process can be daunting for many, as it often involves discussing sensitive issues, potential power dynamics, and the risk of retaliation. However, effectively engaging HR or a supervisor can be an essential step toward resolving conflict and fostering a healthier work environment.

Before seeking assistance from HR or a supervisor, it is vital to understand the specific behavior or incident that prompted the need for support. Being clear about what occurred, the context of the interaction, and its impact on your work or well-being is crucial. A well-defined account helps articulate the situation when discussing it with HR or management, ensuring that the matter is taken seriously and handled appropriately. This preparation can involve documenting specific incidents, noting dates, times, and any witnesses who might corroborate your experience. Such records provide a clear, factual basis for your concerns, which is often necessary when presenting your case to HR or a supervisor.

Additionally, it is essential to reflect on the emotional impact of the behavior. Understanding how the situation has affected you personally can be equally important as the objective details. Rude interactions can lead to feelings of frustration, anxiety, or a decrease in job satisfaction, and conveying these emotions can help HR or your supervisor grasp the severity of the issue. Expressing your feelings provides context and underscores the need for intervention. It illustrates that the behavior is not merely an annoyance but a matter that affects your overall workplace experience.

When approaching HR or a supervisor, timing is crucial. It is advisable to seek support when you feel calm and composed, as this will enable you to articulate your concerns more effectively. Choosing an appropriate setting is equally important; find a private space where you can speak openly without interruptions or distractions. This not only demonstrates professionalism but also respects the sensitivity of the subject matter. If possible, request a meeting in advance, allowing the HR representative or supervisor to prepare for a focused discussion.

During the meeting, present your account of the incidents in a concise and clear manner. Avoid overly emotional language or blaming the other party; instead, focus on "I" statements that express your feelings and experiences. For example, instead of saying, "They are always rude to me," you might say, "I feel uncomfortable when my colleague interrupts me during meetings." This shift in language not only makes the conversation less confrontational but also fosters a collaborative atmosphere for problem-solving.

Active listening is also vital in this dialogue. After presenting your concerns, allow the HR representative or supervisor to respond. They may offer insights, ask clarifying questions, or propose potential solutions. Engaging in this two-way communication demonstrates your willingness to work collaboratively to address the issue. Being open to feedback can also provide additional context for understanding the situation and potential resolutions.

It is important to come to the meeting with an open mind regarding possible solutions. While you may have specific outcomes in mind, be prepared to discuss various approaches that could resolve the conflict. HR or your supervisor may suggest mediation, conflict resolution training, or other interventions that you may not have considered. Showing flexibility can foster a more productive conversation and demonstrate that you are genuinely interested in finding a resolution rather than solely expressing grievances.

If the behavior in question constitutes harassment or a violation of company policy, it is essential to highlight this during your conversation. Many organizations have specific protocols and protections in place for such situations. HR professionals are trained to handle these issues with discretion and may have legal obligations to investigate allegations of harassment or discrimination. Clearly communicating that the behavior has crossed a line can prompt a more serious examination of the matter and ensure that appropriate measures are taken.

Following the initial meeting, it is prudent to follow up with HR or your supervisor regarding the progress of your concerns. This can be done through a brief email or a casual check-in conversation. Expressing gratitude for their attention to the matter and reiterating your interest in a resolution demonstrates professionalism and keeps the lines of communication open. It also emphasizes that you are invested in finding a resolution, which can motivate HR or your supervisor to prioritize your concerns.

In some instances, the response from HR or a supervisor may not meet your expectations. They may not take the necessary actions to address the situation, or their response may seem inadequate to you. In such cases, it is essential to remain persistent. If you feel comfortable, request a follow-up meeting to discuss your concerns further. Articulate why you believe the issue has not been adequately resolved and reiterate the impact it continues to have on your work and well-being. Persistence signals your commitment to the matter and can help hold the organization accountable for addressing employee concerns.

If, after exhausting internal avenues, you feel that your concerns have not been adequately addressed, it may be necessary to explore external options. This could involve seeking advice from legal professionals or consulting with external organizations that specialize in workplace rights. Understanding your rights as an employee can empower you to take further action if needed. In extreme cases, this might involve filing formal complaints with regulatory agencies or considering alternative employment opportunities. However, these steps should generally be viewed as last resorts after all other avenues have been explored.

Another critical aspect of seeking support from HR or a supervisor is understanding the potential for retaliation. It is not uncommon for individuals who report workplace issues to fear negative consequences, such as alienation, further bullying, or even job loss. It is essential to familiarize yourself with your organization's policies on retaliation and to communicate any concerns about this risk during your discussions with HR. Organizations have a responsibility to protect employees from retaliation, and expressing these concerns can help ensure that your rights are upheld.

In addition to addressing immediate concerns, engaging with HR or a supervisor can also contribute to fostering a culture of respect and accountability within the workplace. When employees are empowered to speak up about rude or inappropriate behavior, it sets a precedent for others to do the same. This can lead to an overall decrease in toxic behavior and an increase in workplace morale. By participating in this process, you not only advocate for yourself but also for your colleagues, creating a ripple effect that can contribute to a healthier work environment.

Furthermore, advocating for a supportive workplace culture can be further enhanced by participating in training sessions or workshops offered by HR. Many organizations provide resources to promote effective communication, conflict resolution, and team-building exercises. Engaging in these initiatives can empower you and your colleagues with the tools needed to navigate interpersonal challenges more effectively. Additionally, these programs can foster camaraderie and understanding among team members, contributing to a more cohesive and respectful workplace culture.

Seeking support from HR or a supervisor is a critical step in addressing rude behavior and fostering a healthier workplace environment. By preparing for the conversation, articulating your concerns clearly, and engaging in active listening, you can effectively advocate for yourself while promoting accountability within the organization. While the process may involve challenges, persistence and professionalism can lead to positive outcomes, not just for you but for the entire workplace community. As you navigate these interactions, remember that advocating for a respectful environment ultimately contributes to a culture of collaboration and mutual respect, enhancing both individual well-being and overall organizational success.

CHAPTER 7
THE COMPLAINER

ADDRESSING CHRONIC COMPLAINTS

In any workplace, chronic complaints can create a toxic atmosphere that not only affects the individuals involved but also disrupts the overall morale and productivity of the entire team. Chronic complaints often stem from various sources, including unresolved conflicts, persistent issues with management or colleagues, and a culture that may inadvertently encourage negative behavior. Addressing these complaints is essential for fostering a healthier work environment and ensuring that employees feel heard, valued, and respected.

Chronic complaints typically manifest when individuals express dissatisfaction repeatedly about the same issue without resolution. This can lead to a cycle of negativity, where employees feel powerless to enact change and begin to disengage from their work. The complaining may center on various topics, including management decisions, workload, office politics, or interdepartmental conflicts. The emotional toll of these complaints can be profound, as employees may feel stressed, anxious, or even demoralized when surrounded by a culture of negativity. It is essential to understand that chronic complaints are often a symptom of deeper issues within the workplace, and addressing them requires a nuanced approach.

The first step in addressing chronic complaints is to identify their root causes. Understanding why employees are consistently dissatisfied can provide insights into larger systemic issues that need to be resolved. This may involve conducting anonymous surveys, holding focus groups, or creating open forums for employees to voice their concerns without fear of repercussions. When employees feel safe expressing their grievances, it can lead to valuable feedback that management can use to address underlying issues. The goal is to create a space where employees feel empowered to share their thoughts and concerns, fostering a culture of open communication.

Once the root causes of chronic complaints are identified, it is crucial to develop a plan for addressing these issues effectively. This plan should involve collaboration between management and employees to ensure that everyone is on the same page. For instance, if a common complaint revolves around excessive workloads, management may need to assess staffing levels, redistribute responsibilities, or offer additional training to help employees manage their tasks more effectively. By taking actionable steps to resolve the issues, management can demonstrate a commitment to creating a more positive work environment.

Moreover, addressing chronic complaints involves setting clear expectations for behavior and communication within the workplace. This may include establishing guidelines on how to express concerns constructively and encouraging employees to engage in problem-solving discussions rather than solely venting frustrations. By promoting a proactive approach to communication, employees can learn to address their concerns in a manner that is respectful and conducive to finding solutions. This cultural shift can help reduce the prevalence of chronic complaints over time, as employees will feel more empowered to tackle issues directly rather than resorting to negativity.

It is also important to recognize that chronic complaints can become a self-perpetuating cycle. Employees may feel that their complaints are not being heard or taken seriously, leading them to become more vocal in their dissatisfaction. To break this cycle, management must actively listen to employee concerns and respond appropriately. This may involve acknowledging the complaints, investigating their validity, and providing updates on any actions taken to address the issues. When employees see that their voices matter and that management is committed to making changes, it can foster a sense of trust and engagement that reduces chronic complaints.

In addition to addressing specific complaints, fostering a positive work culture can significantly reduce the frequency of chronic complaints. This may involve promoting teamwork, recognizing employee achievements, and providing opportunities for professional development. When employees feel valued and engaged in their work, they are less likely to focus on negative aspects of the workplace. By creating a culture that emphasizes positivity and support, organizations can reduce the prevalence of chronic complaints and cultivate a more harmonious environment.

Training programs can also play a vital role in addressing chronic complaints. Workshops on communication, conflict resolution, and stress management can equip employees with the skills needed to navigate difficult situations more effectively. Additionally, management should receive training on how to respond to complaints constructively and how to foster an open dialogue with employees. When all employees, including leadership, are equipped with the tools to address issues proactively, the workplace can become more resilient to chronic complaints.

Another essential aspect of addressing chronic complaints is recognizing the importance of follow-up. Once actions have been taken to address specific complaints, it is crucial to monitor the situation and ensure that improvements are sustained over time. This may involve regular check-ins with employees to gauge their satisfaction levels, conducting follow-up surveys, or creating feedback loops that allow employees to share their thoughts on the changes implemented. This ongoing engagement demonstrates a commitment to continuous improvement and can help reinforce a culture of openness and accountability.

In some cases, it may be necessary to address individual employees who are chronic complainers. While it is important to listen to their concerns, it is equally crucial to provide guidance on how to express dissatisfaction constructively. This may involve coaching them on effective communication strategies and encouraging them to focus on solutions rather than merely venting frustrations. In some instances, persistent negativity may indicate deeper issues, such as stress or dissatisfaction with one's role. Addressing these underlying concerns can help individuals re-engage with their work and reduce the frequency of complaints.

Creating a culture of accountability is also essential in addressing chronic complaints. This involves holding employees accountable for their behavior and encouraging them to take responsibility for their actions. For example, if an employee consistently voices complaints but does not participate in finding solutions, it may be necessary to have a candid conversation about their contributions to the workplace culture. Encouraging individuals to take ownership of their complaints and actively participate in problem-solving can help shift the focus from negativity to collaboration.

Moreover, management should lead by example. When leaders demonstrate a positive attitude and proactively address issues, it sets a standard for the rest of the team. Leaders should model effective communication, empathy, and a willingness to listen to feedback. By embodying these values, management can create a ripple effect that encourages employees to adopt similar behaviors, ultimately contributing to a more positive workplace atmosphere.

Recognizing that chronic complaints may sometimes arise from external factors is also crucial. Personal stressors, such as family issues or financial concerns, can spill over into the workplace and contribute to negative attitudes. Management should be aware of this potential influence and consider offering support resources, such as employee assistance programs (EAPs) or mental health resources. Providing access to these services can help employees cope with external stressors and improve their overall well-being, which can, in turn, reduce the frequency of chronic complaints.

Furthermore, fostering a sense of community within the workplace can significantly impact the prevalence of chronic complaints. Team-building activities, social events, and opportunities for employees to connect outside of their usual work responsibilities can help strengthen relationships and create a sense of belonging. When employees feel connected to their colleagues and invested in their work environment, they are more likely to approach issues with a collaborative mindset rather than resorting to chronic complaints.

Addressing chronic complaints in the workplace requires a multifaceted approach that involves understanding root causes, fostering open communication, and promoting a positive work culture. By actively listening to employees, taking actionable steps to resolve issues, and providing training and resources, organizations can reduce the prevalence of chronic complaints and create a more harmonious work environment. Ultimately, cultivating a culture of collaboration and support not only enhances employee satisfaction but also contributes to the overall success and productivity of the organization. By addressing chronic complaints proactively and thoughtfully, employers can create a workplace where employees feel valued, engaged, and empowered to contribute positively to the team dynamic.

SETTING LIMITS ON NEGATIVE CONVERSATIONS

In a professional environment, the nature of conversations can significantly impact the overall atmosphere and productivity. While it's natural for employees to voice concerns or frustrations, there is a fine line between constructive dialogue and negativity. Setting limits on negative conversations is essential for maintaining a healthy workplace culture, ensuring that discussions remain productive and do not devolve into unproductive complaints or toxic interactions. This process involves understanding the dynamics of negative conversations, recognizing their impact on workplace morale, and implementing strategies to redirect discussions in a more positive direction.

Negative conversations often stem from unresolved issues, frustrations with management, or interpersonal conflicts. They can manifest in various forms, including gossip, persistent complaints, and critical remarks that undermine colleagues or the organization as a whole. Such dialogues can create an atmosphere of distrust and disengagement, eroding the foundation of teamwork and collaboration. Recognizing the detrimental effects of these conversations is the first step in addressing them effectively.

One of the key reasons individuals engage in negative conversations is the need for validation or support. Employees may feel overwhelmed or frustrated by their work circumstances and seek out others to share their grievances. While this desire for connection is understandable, it can quickly spiral into a culture of negativity if left unchecked. To mitigate this, it is crucial for both individuals and organizations to set clear boundaries regarding what constitutes acceptable dialogue in the workplace.

Setting limits on negative conversations requires a proactive approach that encourages open communication while discouraging unproductive negativity. A fundamental aspect of this approach is to establish a workplace culture that prioritizes constructive feedback and problem-solving over complaining. Management plays a pivotal role in modeling this behavior, demonstrating how to express concerns in a way that fosters collaboration rather than conflict.

One effective strategy for setting limits is to implement structured communication channels where employees can express their grievances in a productive manner. This could involve regular team meetings dedicated to discussing challenges and brainstorming solutions. By providing a designated space for concerns to be voiced, employees are less likely to engage in off-the-cuff negative conversations that can permeate the workplace. These meetings should be framed as opportunities for collaboration, where team members can work together to identify and address issues collectively.

Another critical aspect of managing negative conversations is to encourage a solution-oriented mindset. When employees approach discussions with a focus on finding solutions rather than merely airing grievances, it shifts the dynamic of the conversation. Managers can guide discussions toward constructive outcomes by asking questions that prompt critical thinking and problem-solving. For instance, instead of allowing a conversation to dwell on a specific issue, a manager might ask, “What do you think we can do to improve this situation?” This simple shift in questioning can help redirect the focus from negativity to action, fostering a more positive dialogue.

In addition to encouraging solution-oriented conversations, it is essential to cultivate emotional intelligence within the team. Understanding and managing one’s emotions, as well as recognizing the emotions of others, can greatly enhance communication effectiveness. Employees who are emotionally intelligent are more likely to navigate difficult conversations with empathy and respect, reducing the likelihood of negativity escalating. Training sessions on emotional intelligence can equip employees with the tools to recognize when a conversation is becoming unproductive and how to steer it back on track.

Moreover, setting clear expectations for communication behavior can be instrumental in minimizing negative conversations. Organizations should define what constitutes unacceptable dialogue and communicate these standards to employees. This may include policies against gossip, personal attacks, or disrespectful remarks. By establishing clear guidelines, employees will have a better understanding of the acceptable boundaries for conversations and can hold each other accountable for adhering to these standards.

It is also important to provide employees with the skills to manage negative conversations when they arise. Training programs on effective communication, conflict resolution, and assertiveness can empower employees to address negativity constructively. For example, employees can learn techniques for redirecting conversations by using phrases like, "I appreciate your perspective, but let's focus on what we can do to improve this situation." This not only helps set limits on negativity but also reinforces a culture of respect and collaboration.

Creating a supportive environment where employees feel safe discussing their concerns is equally vital. When employees know they can voice their grievances without fear of retaliation or judgment, they are more likely to engage in productive conversations. Organizations can foster this sense of safety by promoting open-door policies, encouraging feedback, and demonstrating a genuine commitment to addressing employee concerns. When employees feel valued and heard, they are less likely to engage in negative conversations that undermine morale.

While it's crucial to set limits on negative conversations, it is equally important to recognize the underlying issues that may be contributing to negativity in the workplace. Employees may express dissatisfaction for various reasons, including heavy workloads, lack of recognition, or unresolved conflicts. Addressing these root causes proactively can significantly reduce the frequency of negative conversations. Managers should regularly check in with employees to gauge their satisfaction levels and offer support where needed. By taking the time to understand employees' concerns and challenges, management can create an environment where negativity is less likely to flourish.

Another effective strategy for minimizing negative conversations is to focus on celebrating successes and recognizing achievements within the team. When employees feel appreciated and acknowledged for their contributions, they are more likely to adopt a positive outlook. Regularly highlighting individual and team accomplishments can foster a sense of camaraderie and motivation, reducing the likelihood of negativity taking hold. Implementing recognition programs, team-building activities, or simply taking the time to express gratitude can go a long way in promoting a positive workplace culture.

It's also essential to acknowledge that some negativity may be rooted in personal factors outside of work. Employees may face challenges in their personal lives that spill over into their work attitudes and conversations. While it is important to maintain boundaries, offering resources such as employee assistance programs (EAPs) can provide support for employees dealing with external stressors. When employees feel supported in their overall well-being, they are more likely to engage positively with their colleagues.

In instances where negative conversations persist despite efforts to set limits, it may be necessary to address the behavior of individuals directly. This can be a challenging conversation but is crucial for maintaining a healthy workplace environment. Managers should approach these discussions with empathy and a focus on improvement rather than punishment. For example, a manager might say, "I've noticed that our discussions often focus on negative aspects. How can we work together to shift the focus toward solutions?" This approach not only addresses the issue but also invites the individual to participate in finding a way forward.

Setting limits on negative conversations is not a one-time effort but an ongoing process that requires commitment from all levels of the organization. It involves fostering a culture of respect, collaboration, and accountability while providing employees with the tools to communicate effectively. As employees learn to express their concerns constructively and engage in solution-oriented dialogues, the overall atmosphere of the workplace can shift dramatically. Over time, organizations can cultivate an environment where negative conversations are minimized, and employees feel empowered to contribute positively to their teams.

The impact of negative conversations in the workplace cannot be underestimated. By proactively setting limits on these dialogues, organizations can create a more positive and productive environment for their employees. Through structured communication channels, a focus on solutions, emotional intelligence training, and clear expectations, teams can redirect negativity into constructive discussions. Moreover, by acknowledging and addressing underlying issues, celebrating successes, and providing support, organizations can foster a culture of collaboration and respect. Ultimately, setting limits on negative conversations is a vital step toward building a thriving workplace where employees feel valued, engaged, and motivated to contribute to the collective success of the team.

OFFERING CONSTRUCTIVE SOLUTIONS

In any workplace, addressing conflict and negativity effectively is crucial for fostering a healthy and productive environment. One of the most constructive approaches to managing rude or difficult interactions is to focus on offering constructive solutions rather than getting mired in the negativity that often accompanies such exchanges. This method not only diffuses tension but also promotes collaboration, respect, and a problem-solving mindset among colleagues. Understanding how to present constructive solutions effectively involves mastering communication techniques, embracing empathy, and cultivating an atmosphere that values constructive dialogue.

At the heart of offering constructive solutions is the recognition that many rude or difficult interactions stem from frustrations, misunderstandings, or unmet needs. When individuals feel unheard or undervalued, they may resort to rudeness as a way to express their dissatisfaction. By reframing the focus of conversations toward constructive solutions, one can create an opportunity for dialogue that encourages all parties to move beyond their grievances and work together toward a positive outcome. This shift in perspective is essential for maintaining professionalism and promoting a collaborative workplace culture.

When faced with a rude or challenging comment, it is vital first to pause and assess the situation. Taking a moment to breathe and reflect can help prevent a knee-jerk defensive response. Acknowledging the emotion behind the rudeness—whether it be frustration, stress, or another underlying issue—can help frame your response. For example, if a colleague snaps at you during a meeting, instead of reacting defensively, consider that they may be overwhelmed with their workload or dealing with personal issues. By recognizing their emotional state, you can approach the conversation with greater empathy and understanding.

Empathy plays a crucial role in diffusing tension and creating an environment where constructive solutions can flourish. When responding to rudeness, consider the following framework: acknowledge the person's feelings, validate their concerns, and then pivot the conversation toward solutions. For instance, if someone expresses frustration about a project delay, you might say, "I understand that you're feeling frustrated about the timeline. Let's work together to figure out how we can get back on track." This response validates their feelings while simultaneously redirecting the conversation toward actionable steps.

Another key aspect of offering constructive solutions is to maintain a focus on the problem at hand rather than making it personal. Avoid engaging in blame or accusations; instead, concentrate on the issue itself and how it can be resolved. For example, if a coworker criticizes your work during a discussion, resist the urge to respond defensively. Instead, ask clarifying questions about their concerns, which can help shift the focus away from personal criticism and toward the specific aspects of the project that require improvement. By emphasizing a collaborative approach, you create an atmosphere conducive to constructive dialogue.

It's also essential to encourage open communication when discussing solutions. Inviting the other party to share their thoughts and suggestions not only helps them feel valued but can also lead to innovative ideas that may not have been considered otherwise. When individuals feel that their input is appreciated, they are more likely to engage positively in the conversation. You might say something like, "What do you think could help us move forward on this project?" This invites collaboration and demonstrates that you are committed to finding a solution together.

Furthermore, providing constructive solutions requires a certain level of preparedness. Anticipate potential challenges or objections that may arise during the discussion and be ready to address them thoughtfully. This means doing your homework and having relevant information at hand. For instance, if a team member is frustrated with the current project management tools, you could research alternative options and present them during the conversation. By arriving equipped with knowledge and potential solutions, you signal your commitment to resolving the issue and encourage others to adopt a similar mindset.

In many cases, presenting solutions is about framing the conversation in a way that highlights the benefits of collaboration. Rather than merely presenting a list of options, communicate how these solutions can positively impact the team or project outcomes. For example, if you suggest a change in a process, explain how it could lead to greater efficiency or improved communication. This positive framing not only makes your proposals more compelling but also helps others see the value in working together toward a common goal.

It is also essential to approach constructive solutions with a mindset of flexibility. Be open to feedback and willing to adjust your proposals based on the input of others. Rigidly adhering to your ideas can stifle collaboration and breed resentment, while demonstrating a willingness to adapt fosters a sense of shared ownership in the resolution process. If your initial solution is met with resistance, ask for suggestions on how to improve it. This not only shows respect for others' opinions but also encourages a more inclusive approach to problem-solving.

Moreover, timing can be a crucial factor in offering constructive solutions. Sometimes, emotions may run high, making it challenging to have productive discussions. If you sense that a conversation may lead to further conflict, consider pausing the discussion until all parties are calmer and more receptive. Communicate your intention to revisit the topic later when everyone is in a better frame of mind. This demonstrates respect for everyone involved and allows for a more thoughtful exploration of solutions.

In addition to focusing on immediate solutions, consider the long-term implications of your discussions. Establishing a culture of constructive feedback and solution-oriented communication can lead to lasting positive change in the workplace. Encourage regular check-ins or team meetings where everyone is invited to share challenges and collaboratively brainstorm solutions. This ongoing practice not only reinforces a collective commitment to problem-solving but also builds trust among team members, reducing the likelihood of rudeness arising from unresolved issues in the future.

Training and development initiatives can also play a significant role in equipping employees with the skills necessary for effective communication and problem-solving. Workshops or seminars focused on conflict resolution, active listening, and emotional intelligence can empower team members to approach difficult conversations with confidence. When employees feel equipped to handle conflicts constructively, they are less likely to resort to rudeness or negativity in their interactions.

It is important to remember that offering constructive solutions is not about suppressing emotions or pretending that problems don't exist. Instead, it is about addressing those problems head-on in a respectful and collaborative manner. Acknowledging the reality of the situation while focusing on ways to improve it is key to fostering a positive workplace culture. When employees feel safe to express their frustrations while simultaneously engaging in solution-oriented discussions, the overall atmosphere of the workplace becomes more productive and supportive.

The power of appreciation and recognition cannot be overlooked when discussing constructive solutions. Acknowledging the contributions and efforts of colleagues during the problem-solving process reinforces a culture of collaboration. When team members feel valued for their input, they are more likely to engage positively and supportively in future discussions. Make it a practice to express gratitude for colleagues' contributions, whether through informal acknowledgments in meetings or more formal recognition programs.

Offering constructive solutions in response to rudeness or negativity in the workplace is a powerful strategy for fostering a positive environment. By reframing conversations around empathy, collaboration, and problem-solving, individuals can diffuse tension and redirect discussions toward actionable outcomes. Creating a culture that values constructive dialogue, encouraging open communication, and equipping employees with the skills to address conflicts effectively are vital components of this approach. Ultimately, when employees are empowered to engage in constructive conversations, the workplace becomes a more supportive and productive space where everyone can thrive.

CHAPTER 8

THE PASSIVE-AGGRESSIVE PERSON

UNDERSTANDING PASSIVE-AGGRESSIVE BEHAVIOR

Understanding passive-aggressive behavior is crucial for navigating interpersonal dynamics, particularly in workplace settings where collaboration and teamwork are essential. Passive-aggressive behavior manifests as indirect resistance to demands or expectations, often leading to misunderstandings, frustration, and conflicts. Recognizing the subtleties of this behavior can enhance communication and promote a healthier work environment.

At its core, passive-aggressive behavior stems from a conflict between the individual's feelings and their inability to express those feelings directly. This often results in behaviors that appear benign on the surface but carry underlying hostility or resentment. Individuals exhibiting passive-aggressive tendencies may find it challenging to express their anger or dissatisfaction openly due to fear of confrontation, a desire to avoid conflict, or a belief that direct communication is inappropriate. Instead, they resort to indirect means of expressing their discontent, which can include sarcasm, procrastination, sullenness, or intentionally ambiguous communication.

One of the most common scenarios where passive-aggressive behavior occurs is in response to authority or perceived control. For instance, an employee may feel overwhelmed by their workload and may be frustrated with their supervisor for assigning additional tasks. Instead of openly discussing their feelings, the employee might agree to take on the extra responsibilities while subtly undermining their efforts by delaying completion or producing subpar work. This indirect approach allows the individual to avoid direct conflict while simultaneously expressing their dissatisfaction through non-verbal cues or indirect actions.

Recognizing passive-aggressive behavior requires an awareness of its manifestations. Often, those displaying such behavior may employ sarcastic remarks disguised as jokes. For instance, an employee might say, "Oh, I'm sure this will be easy for you since you're so good at everything," which appears humorous but actually conveys resentment toward the colleague's competence. This type of communication can create confusion, as the recipient may struggle to discern whether the comment is playful banter or a veiled attack.

Another common form of passive-aggressive behavior is the use of procrastination as a weapon. When faced with a task they dislike, an individual may delay its completion, citing other pressing matters as an excuse. This behavior can lead to frustration for team members who rely on the completion of that task for their own responsibilities. Such delays may not only impact productivity but also create tension among colleagues, leading to a toxic work environment.

It is also important to consider the role of non-verbal communication in passive-aggressive interactions. Body language, facial expressions, and tone of voice can reveal underlying feelings that contradict the words being spoken. For instance, a person may say, "I'm fine," while crossing their arms and avoiding eye contact, indicating that they are, in fact, anything but fine. This disconnect between verbal and non-verbal communication can create misunderstandings and foster an environment where open dialogue is stifled.

Understanding the motivations behind passive-aggressive behavior is essential for addressing it effectively. Often, individuals who engage in such behavior may lack the tools or confidence to communicate their needs assertively. They may fear the repercussions of expressing their feelings directly, leading them to resort to indirect methods that ultimately harm relationships. Building emotional intelligence and communication skills can help individuals recognize their patterns and seek healthier ways to express themselves.

In the workplace, passive-aggressive behavior can have significant repercussions, not only for the individuals involved but also for the team as a whole. When such behaviors go unaddressed, they can lead to decreased morale, increased stress, and lower productivity. Team members may become hesitant to communicate openly, fearing backlash or further passive-aggressive remarks. This cycle of avoidance and indirect hostility can erode trust and collaboration, ultimately hindering the team's ability to function effectively.

Addressing passive-aggressive behavior requires a multifaceted approach. First, it is important to create an environment that encourages open and honest communication. This can be achieved by fostering a culture of psychological safety, where team members feel secure in expressing their thoughts and feelings without fear of reprisal. Leaders can model this behavior by openly discussing their own challenges and encouraging others to do the same. When individuals feel comfortable sharing their concerns, they are less likely to resort to passive-aggressive tactics.

Another effective strategy for addressing passive-aggressive behavior is to engage in active listening. When someone expresses dissatisfaction, it is essential to listen without judgment and validate their feelings. This involves acknowledging the individual's perspective, even if it differs from your own. By demonstrating empathy and understanding, you can help the person feel heard, which may reduce their inclination to express their frustration through passive-aggressive means.

In situations where passive-aggressive behavior becomes evident, it is crucial to address it directly but tactfully. Initiating a conversation with the individual in question can provide an opportunity to clarify intentions and address any misunderstandings. It is essential to approach the conversation with a non-confrontational demeanor, using "I" statements to express how their behavior impacts you and the team. For instance, instead of saying, "You always procrastinate on this task," you could say, "I feel frustrated when deadlines are missed because it affects our overall progress." This approach helps to keep the focus on the behavior rather than personalizing the issue, making it easier for the individual to engage in constructive dialogue.

It is also valuable to encourage the individual exhibiting passive-aggressive behavior to explore their feelings and motivations. Creating a safe space for them to express their frustrations can help them understand the root causes of their behavior. Engaging in reflective conversations may reveal underlying issues such as fear of failure, lack of assertiveness, or a desire to be heard. By addressing these issues, you can assist the individual in developing healthier coping mechanisms and communication strategies.

Furthermore, providing training and resources on effective communication skills can empower employees to express their needs and concerns more assertively. Workshops on conflict resolution, emotional intelligence, and active listening can equip team members with the tools necessary to navigate difficult conversations. By fostering a culture of open communication and collaboration, you can mitigate the prevalence of passive-aggressive behavior and create a more harmonious workplace.

Additionally, setting clear expectations and accountability can help reduce the likelihood of passive-aggressive behavior. Establishing specific goals, deadlines, and responsibilities ensures that team members understand their roles and the importance of meeting commitments. When expectations are clearly communicated, individuals are less likely to resort to indirect methods of expressing dissatisfaction, as they understand the consequences of their actions.

Understanding passive-aggressive behavior is essential for fostering effective communication and collaboration in the workplace. Recognizing the signs of this behavior and its underlying motivations can empower individuals to address conflicts constructively. By promoting a culture of open dialogue, active listening, and assertive communication, organizations can create an environment where team members feel valued and respected. Ultimately, addressing passive-aggressive behavior not only enhances individual relationships but also contributes to a more productive and positive work environment for all.

DIRECT COMMUNICATION TECHNIQUES

Direct communication techniques are essential tools in the workplace, enabling individuals to convey their thoughts, feelings, and expectations clearly and effectively. In environments where interactions can become heated or contentious, mastering these techniques can prevent misunderstandings, foster positive relationships, and promote a culture of openness. When faced with rudeness or challenging conversations, employing direct communication strategies can significantly impact the outcome of interactions, creating a space for constructive dialogue rather than escalating tension.

At the heart of direct communication is the principle of clarity. Clear communication entails expressing thoughts and feelings succinctly, avoiding ambiguous language, and ensuring that the intended message is delivered without room for misinterpretation. This requires an understanding of one's emotions and the ability to articulate them effectively. For instance, when a colleague makes a dismissive remark, instead of reacting defensively or with sarcasm, a person practicing direct communication might calmly state, "I felt overlooked when you dismissed my suggestion in the meeting. I believe my input could have contributed positively." This approach not only clarifies the speaker's feelings but also invites dialogue, as it encourages the other person to reflect on their behavior.

Another fundamental aspect of direct communication is using "I" statements instead of "you" statements. "I" statements focus on the speaker's feelings and experiences rather than placing blame on the other person. For example, rather than saying, "You always interrupt me," which can be perceived as accusatory, one might say, "I feel frustrated when I am interrupted during discussions." This subtle shift in language can reduce defensiveness in the other person, making them more receptive to the feedback being given. It transforms the conversation from one of blame to one of personal experience, paving the way for a more meaningful exchange.

Active listening is an indispensable technique that complements direct communication. It involves fully engaging with the speaker, both verbally and non-verbally, to ensure that their message is understood. Active listening requires maintaining eye contact, nodding in acknowledgment, and providing verbal affirmations, such as "I see" or "That makes sense." Additionally, it involves paraphrasing what the other person has said to confirm understanding. For example, if a colleague expresses frustration about a project deadline, a listener might respond with, "So, you're saying that the timeline is unrealistic given the resources we have?" This demonstrates attentiveness and validates the speaker's feelings, creating a collaborative atmosphere that encourages further discussion.

Furthermore, direct communication also hinges on the importance of timing and environment. Engaging in difficult conversations in an appropriate setting can greatly influence the effectiveness of the communication. Ideally, discussions about sensitive topics should take place in a private, neutral environment where both parties feel comfortable expressing themselves without distractions or interruptions. Timing is equally important; approaching a colleague immediately after a heated moment may not yield the best results. Instead, allowing time for emotions to settle can lead to a more productive conversation. For example, if an argument arises during a team meeting, it may be more effective to suggest a follow-up conversation later, thereby providing both individuals the chance to reflect on the situation.

Moreover, preparation plays a vital role in successful direct communication. Anticipating potential responses and formulating one's own replies can help keep the conversation on track and prevent it from veering into hostility. Preparing for a conversation may involve jotting down key points, practicing what to say, and considering the other person's perspective. This proactive approach not only helps the speaker feel more confident but also reinforces the message's clarity and intention. When confronting a colleague about their inappropriate comments, for example, having specific instances in mind can help articulate the concern without getting sidetracked by emotions.

Direct communication techniques also encourage individuals to express their needs and set boundaries assertively. Assertiveness is a crucial component of effective communication, as it allows individuals to stand up for their rights while respecting the rights of others. Being assertive involves expressing one's feelings, needs, and preferences confidently and directly, without resorting to aggression or passivity. For example, if a team member consistently takes credit for a shared project, an assertive response could be, "I would appreciate it if we could ensure that credit is shared among all contributors in future discussions." This communicates the need for acknowledgment without attacking the other person's character, thus fostering an environment of mutual respect.

The power of body language and tone cannot be underestimated in direct communication. Non-verbal cues such as posture, gestures, and facial expressions can significantly influence how a message is received. Maintaining an open posture, using appropriate gestures, and ensuring that facial expressions align with verbal messages can enhance the effectiveness of communication. For example, a warm smile and an open stance can help diffuse tension and invite collaboration, whereas crossed arms or a furrowed brow may communicate defensiveness or hostility. Additionally, the tone of voice conveys emotions that words alone may not express. A calm, steady tone can help maintain a productive atmosphere, while a raised voice can escalate tensions and shut down dialogue.

Understanding the other person's perspective is also key to effective direct communication. Empathy involves recognizing and validating the feelings and experiences of others, which can foster understanding and cooperation. When a colleague is upset about a project change, acknowledging their feelings by saying, "I can see this change is frustrating for you, and I understand why you might feel that way," can help bridge the gap between differing perspectives. This acknowledgment can facilitate a more open exchange of ideas and lead to finding a mutually agreeable solution.

Additionally, direct communication should be solution-oriented rather than focused solely on problems. When conflicts arise, it is important to approach discussions with a mindset geared toward finding constructive solutions. Instead of dwelling on what went wrong or assigning blame, individuals can steer conversations toward identifying ways to move forward. For instance, if two team members disagree about a project's direction, they can frame the conversation by asking, "What are some options we can explore to address both our concerns and achieve our goals?" This forward-thinking approach fosters collaboration and problem-solving, ultimately strengthening team dynamics.

Furthermore, practicing self-regulation during challenging conversations is essential for maintaining effective direct communication. It is natural to feel emotional when confronted with rudeness or negativity, but allowing those emotions to dictate responses can lead to counterproductive outcomes. Developing strategies for managing emotions, such as deep breathing, pausing before responding, or taking a moment to collect thoughts, can help individuals respond more rationally rather than reactively. For example, if a colleague responds to feedback with defensiveness, taking a deep breath before responding can help prevent escalation and allow for a more thoughtful dialogue.

In cases where direct communication does not yield the desired outcome, it may be necessary to involve a third party or seek mediation. This approach can provide a neutral perspective and facilitate a more productive conversation. When emotions run high, having a mediator can help guide the discussion, ensuring that both parties feel heard and understood. Mediators can also assist in identifying common ground and establishing actionable steps for resolution. Seeking support from a supervisor or HR representative can be beneficial in navigating particularly challenging situations, ensuring that all parties are held accountable for their behavior and communication.

Ultimately, mastering direct communication techniques empowers individuals to engage in meaningful interactions, navigate conflicts effectively, and foster a positive workplace culture. These skills are not only essential for addressing rudeness or challenging conversations but also contribute to building stronger relationships and enhancing overall team dynamics. As individuals become more proficient in direct communication, they create a ripple effect, encouraging colleagues to embrace similar approaches and cultivate an environment of respect, collaboration, and understanding.

The ability to communicate directly and effectively is a vital skill in any workplace setting. By implementing techniques such as using “I” statements, practicing active listening, preparing for conversations, and maintaining an assertive yet respectful demeanor, individuals can navigate difficult discussions with confidence. By fostering an environment where open dialogue and mutual respect are prioritized, organizations can enhance teamwork and productivity, ultimately leading to greater success and satisfaction among all employees. Embracing direct communication is not just a strategy for addressing rudeness; it is a pathway to a healthier, more collaborative workplace.

SETTING CLEAR EXPECTATIONS

Setting clear expectations is a cornerstone of effective communication, especially in workplace environments where misunderstandings and misinterpretations can lead to conflict and tension. When interactions turn negative, it is often a result of unclear or uncommunicated expectations. By establishing clear guidelines and parameters for behavior and performance, individuals can significantly reduce the likelihood of rudeness and miscommunication, paving the way for more respectful and productive exchanges.

To begin with, setting clear expectations involves understanding the context in which you are operating. Each workplace has its own culture, norms, and dynamics that influence how people communicate and interact with one another. Acknowledging these factors is essential to framing your expectations in a way that resonates with those around you. For example, in a fast-paced corporate environment, the expectation of prompt communication and quick decision-making may be necessary. However, in a more relaxed creative setting, the emphasis might be on collaboration and open-ended discussions. By aligning expectations with the workplace culture, individuals can create a more cohesive atmosphere where everyone is on the same page.

A fundamental aspect of setting expectations is clarity. This means articulating what you want and need from others in a straightforward manner. Vague requests or ambiguous statements can lead to confusion and frustration, often resulting in unintended rudeness or conflict. For instance, if a manager asks their team to "work harder," the lack of specificity can lead to various interpretations. Instead, a clear expectation might be: "I would like everyone to increase their output by 20% over the next quarter while maintaining our quality standards." This specificity removes ambiguity, giving team members a concrete target to aim for and thus minimizing the chances of miscommunication.

Furthermore, when expressing expectations, it is crucial to communicate not only the desired outcomes but also the reasons behind them. Understanding the "why" can foster a sense of purpose and motivation among team members. When individuals comprehend the rationale for certain expectations, they are more likely to engage positively with them. For example, if a supervisor implements a new reporting structure, explaining that it is intended to improve workflow efficiency and enhance transparency can help employees appreciate the change rather than resist it. This approach helps cultivate an environment of trust and respect, as employees feel that their leaders are open and honest about their intentions.

Another important element of setting clear expectations is ensuring that they are mutually agreed upon. This process should be collaborative rather than unilateral, promoting a sense of ownership and accountability among team members. When expectations are set in consultation with those who will be affected by them, individuals are more likely to feel invested in the outcomes. For instance, during team meetings, discussing project timelines and individual roles can lead to collective agreement on deliverables. This collaboration allows for the incorporation of different perspectives and fosters an environment where everyone feels their voice is heard.

Regularly revisiting and reinforcing expectations is another key practice in maintaining clarity. As projects evolve and circumstances change, it is essential to ensure that everyone remains aligned with the established expectations. Periodic check-ins can serve as reminders, allowing team members to discuss any challenges they may face in meeting expectations and adjusting them as necessary. For example, if a team member struggles to meet a deadline due to unforeseen circumstances, a discussion can lead to a renegotiation of expectations that acknowledges the reality of the situation while still aiming for accountability. This flexibility encourages resilience and adaptability, creating a culture that values growth and collaboration.

Additionally, using a variety of communication channels can enhance the clarity of expectations. While verbal communication is essential, supplementing it with written documentation ensures that there is a record of what has been discussed and agreed upon. Email summaries, shared project management tools, or even visual aids like charts and diagrams can all serve as reminders of expectations. This multi-faceted approach caters to different learning styles and reinforces the messages being conveyed, helping to eliminate any ambiguity. When expectations are documented, it also provides a reference point for future discussions, creating a transparent and accountable environment.

Furthermore, encouraging feedback is critical to the process of setting expectations. Individuals should feel comfortable expressing their thoughts, concerns, or suggestions regarding the expectations that have been laid out. This two-way communication fosters a sense of belonging and empowerment, allowing team members to voice any challenges they may encounter. By inviting feedback, leaders demonstrate that they value input and are willing to adapt expectations based on the needs and realities of their team.

For instance, if an employee feels that a target is unrealistic due to workload constraints, discussing this feedback openly can lead to adjustments that ensure both accountability and well-being.

It is also important to recognize that expectations should be realistic and attainable. Setting the bar too high can lead to frustration and disengagement, while setting it too low may result in complacency. Striking a balance between challenging and achievable expectations is crucial. Utilizing the SMART criteria—Specific, Measurable, Achievable, Relevant, and Time-bound—can guide leaders in formulating expectations that are both realistic and motivating. For example, instead of saying, "I want you to improve your performance," a SMART expectation could be, "I want you to complete three client proposals by the end of the month, focusing on quality and client needs." This specificity provides a clear framework that individuals can strive to meet.

Moreover, it is vital to recognize and celebrate successes as expectations are met. Acknowledgment of achievements reinforces positive behavior and motivates individuals to continue striving toward established expectations. Celebrating milestones, whether big or small, creates a positive feedback loop that encourages individuals to engage more actively with their work. For instance, when a team successfully meets a project deadline, acknowledging their effort through a team lunch or a simple "thank you" can boost morale and foster a culture of appreciation. When individuals feel valued for their contributions, they are more likely to maintain a respectful and collaborative approach in their interactions with others.

Additionally, clear expectations help to set the tone for how individuals communicate with one another. When expectations are established around respectful communication, individuals are less likely to engage in rudeness or hostility. For example, if a team agrees to approach conflicts with the intent of finding solutions rather than assigning blame, this expectation creates a foundation for constructive conversations. Individuals are more likely to address challenges directly and tactfully, fostering a culture of respect and open dialogue.

Furthermore, leaders must model the behavior they expect from their teams. If a manager sets clear expectations but fails to adhere to them in their own communication and actions, it undermines the established guidelines. Consistency in behavior is essential to reinforcing expectations; leaders must exemplify the standards they expect others to uphold. This modeling fosters credibility and respect, encouraging team members to emulate the desired behavior. For instance, if a manager commits to providing timely feedback, they must consistently follow through to establish a culture of accountability.

In the face of rudeness or challenging interactions, setting clear expectations can act as a protective barrier, providing individuals with the tools to respond appropriately. When expectations around communication and behavior are well-defined, individuals are less likely to feel caught off guard when faced with negativity. For instance, if a team has established the expectation of addressing conflicts openly and respectfully, an individual encountering rudeness can refer back to these guidelines when formulating their response. This grounding in shared expectations empowers individuals to remain calm and assertive, even in challenging situations.

Lastly, it is essential to remember that setting clear expectations is an ongoing process. As teams evolve, new members join, and projects change, expectations may need to be revisited and revised. Flexibility is key; while clarity is paramount, rigidity can stifle creativity and innovation. By remaining open to adapting expectations based on the changing dynamics of the team, individuals create an environment where collaboration thrives. Embracing this adaptability fosters a culture of continuous improvement, where team members feel encouraged to evolve and grow together.

Setting clear expectations is an essential practice that lays the groundwork for effective communication and respectful interactions in the workplace. By establishing clarity, promoting collaboration, encouraging feedback, and modeling desired behaviors, individuals can significantly reduce misunderstandings and conflicts. The commitment to clear expectations fosters an environment of trust, accountability, and respect, ultimately leading to a more harmonious and productive workplace. In a world where rudeness and negativity can easily arise, the proactive approach of setting clear expectations serves as a vital tool for cultivating positive relationships and constructive dialogue. Embracing this practice not only enhances individual interactions but also contributes to a healthier organizational culture overall.

CHAPTER 9

THE DIFFICULT BOSS

DEALING WITH A DIFFICULT SUPERIOR

Navigating the complexities of workplace dynamics can be particularly challenging when it comes to dealing with a difficult superior. Whether the issue arises from their communication style, leadership approach, or personal behavior, the impact of a difficult superior can be profound. It can lead to increased stress, lowered morale, and diminished productivity. Learning how to effectively manage these situations is crucial for both professional success and personal well-being. This journey begins with understanding the nature of the difficulties faced and then developing strategies to address them.

First and foremost, it is essential to recognize that difficult behavior often stems from various underlying factors. A superior may be under pressure to meet deadlines, face organizational changes, or navigate their own interpersonal issues. These stressors can manifest as irritability, impatience, or a lack of empathy in their interactions. Understanding this context can provide valuable insight and foster empathy, allowing for a more compassionate approach to the relationship. When viewing a superior's difficult behavior through this lens, it becomes possible to respond not just to the behavior itself, but also to the human emotions behind it.

One of the first steps in dealing with a difficult superior is to assess your own responses. Personal reactions can vary widely; some individuals may feel anger, frustration, or helplessness, while others may withdraw or comply. It is vital to take stock of these feelings and consider how they influence interactions with the superior. Being aware of one's emotional triggers can help in formulating a more constructive response rather than reacting impulsively. For instance, if criticism from a superior tends to provoke defensiveness, it may be beneficial to practice self-regulation techniques, such as deep breathing or pausing before responding, to ensure that responses are measured and thoughtful.

Establishing clear and open lines of communication is critical when managing a relationship with a difficult superior. Often, misunderstandings can escalate into conflicts simply due to a lack of effective communication. When addressing issues or concerns, it is advisable to approach the superior with a mindset focused on collaboration rather than confrontation. Framing discussions around common goals can help bridge gaps and foster a sense of teamwork. For example, instead of saying, “You never listen to my ideas,” a more constructive approach might be, “I believe we can enhance our project by discussing ideas together. Can we schedule some time to brainstorm?” This type of language emphasizes partnership and reduces the likelihood of defensiveness.

In addition to improving communication, it is also important to clarify expectations and seek alignment on objectives. A difficult superior may have a different vision or set of priorities that are not immediately apparent. Initiating a conversation to discuss goals, deadlines, and performance metrics can align both parties and reduce ambiguity. By asking questions like, “What are your key priorities for this project?” or “How do you envision my role contributing to our success?” one can gain insights into the superior’s perspective while also establishing a foundation for mutual understanding. This proactive approach helps to ensure that both parties are on the same page and working toward a common objective.

Moreover, providing feedback to a difficult superior can be a delicate task, but it is essential for maintaining a healthy working relationship. If the superior's behavior is impacting your work or the team's dynamics, it may be necessary to share your perspective. However, it is crucial to frame this feedback constructively. Using "I" statements can help express how their behavior affects you without sounding accusatory. For instance, saying "I feel overwhelmed when the expectations are unclear" rather than "You never communicate properly" can prevent defensive reactions and foster a more open dialogue. When providing feedback, it is also vital to offer potential solutions or alternatives, demonstrating that you are invested in the team's success and not simply pointing out flaws.

Building rapport with a difficult superior can serve as an effective strategy to mitigate challenging interactions. Taking the time to understand their preferences, interests, and communication styles can create a more positive atmosphere. Engaging in small talk or showing genuine interest in their experiences can break down barriers and foster a sense of connection. For instance, if a superior enjoys discussing industry trends or sharing personal anecdotes, leveraging these topics can lead to more relaxed and productive conversations. As rapport develops, difficult interactions may become less frequent and more manageable, creating a more constructive work environment.

It is also beneficial to document interactions with a difficult superior. Keeping a record of conversations, feedback received, and any incidents of difficult behavior can serve as a reference point for future discussions. This documentation can be particularly valuable when addressing patterns of behavior that may need to be discussed more formally. If there is a need to escalate issues to HR or upper management, having detailed records can provide necessary context and evidence to support your concerns. Documenting interactions can also aid in clarifying your own thoughts and feelings, allowing you to approach discussions with greater confidence.

When faced with a difficult superior, it is essential to establish boundaries to protect one's well-being. While it is important to be flexible and understanding, it is equally crucial to maintain a sense of self-respect and professionalism. If a superior consistently engages in behaviors that are disrespectful or inappropriate, addressing these issues directly may be necessary. For instance, if a superior raises their voice during discussions, calmly stating, “I prefer to discuss issues in a more respectful manner; it helps me focus better,” can set a boundary while encouraging a more constructive approach to communication. Setting boundaries helps ensure that interactions remain professional and respectful, creating a healthier work environment.

In the process of managing a relationship with a difficult superior, it is also vital to cultivate resilience and self-care. Dealing with challenging personalities can be draining, and taking care of your mental and emotional health is paramount. Practicing stress management techniques, such as mindfulness, exercise, or seeking support from friends and family, can help mitigate the impact of a difficult superior's behavior. Engaging in regular self-reflection can also foster personal growth and enhance emotional intelligence, enabling better navigation of workplace challenges. Ultimately, prioritizing self-care empowers individuals to remain composed and focused, even in the face of adversity.

If challenges persist and impact your professional experience significantly, it may be necessary to consider involving HR or seeking support from other resources within the organization. HR departments can offer guidance on navigating difficult relationships and may facilitate discussions between employees and management to address conflicts. If direct communication does not yield positive results, involving a neutral third party can provide a fresh perspective and promote resolution. It is essential to approach this process with care, ensuring that any actions taken align with organizational policies and procedures.

Furthermore, it is important to recognize when the situation may not be salvageable. In some cases, the behavior of a difficult superior may not improve despite your best efforts. If the relationship continues to cause undue stress or negatively impacts your performance and well-being, it may be necessary to explore alternative options within the organization or seek new employment opportunities. Prioritizing your mental health and career satisfaction is vital, and sometimes, the best course of action involves seeking a healthier work environment.

Developing assertiveness is another key aspect of dealing with a difficult superior. Assertiveness allows individuals to express their needs and opinions confidently while respecting others. Practicing assertive communication involves using clear and direct language, maintaining eye contact, and being mindful of body language. For example, when addressing a disagreement or concern with a superior, using phrases like "I would like to discuss this further" or "I believe there is a more effective way to approach this" can convey assertiveness while remaining respectful. Developing assertiveness fosters confidence and empowers individuals to engage in constructive discussions.

Learning to manage conflict effectively is essential when dealing with a difficult superior. Conflicts may arise due to differing opinions, communication styles, or workplace dynamics. Approaching conflicts with a problem-solving mindset can lead to more productive outcomes. Rather than viewing conflict as a threat, reframing it as an opportunity for growth and improvement can facilitate positive change. Focusing on solutions rather than assigning blame can create an environment conducive to collaboration and teamwork. When approaching conflicts with a collaborative mindset, individuals can foster more respectful interactions and improve relationships.

Dealing with a difficult superior requires a multifaceted approach that includes understanding the underlying dynamics, fostering effective communication, establishing clear expectations, and building rapport. Documenting interactions, setting boundaries, and prioritizing self-care are essential practices for maintaining well-being while navigating challenging relationships. Developing assertiveness and conflict management skills further empowers individuals to engage in constructive discussions and promote positive change. Ultimately, the journey of managing a relationship with a difficult superior is one of growth, resilience, and empowerment, leading to more fulfilling professional experiences.

DOCUMENTING ISSUES

Documenting issues in the workplace is a critical skill that can significantly affect how conflicts and difficult interactions are navigated. The ability to accurately record and report incidents involving rude behavior, harassment, or any form of unprofessional conduct is invaluable. It not only helps in resolving disputes but also serves to protect one's own interests and well-being in a professional environment. Documentation becomes particularly important when dealing with recurring problems or when escalation becomes necessary.

At its core, documentation involves keeping a detailed and systematic account of specific interactions or incidents that occur in the workplace. This can include anything from rude remarks made by a colleague to inappropriate feedback from a supervisor. The goal is to create a comprehensive record that is factual, objective, and devoid of emotional bias. This record can then be utilized for various purposes, including discussions with HR, management, or as evidence if formal actions are needed.

The first step in effective documentation is recognizing what constitutes a documentable incident. This can vary widely depending on the workplace culture and the nature of the behavior being addressed. Generally, any interaction that is rude, disrespectful, or violates company policy should be noted. This could encompass verbal abuse, bullying, passive-aggressive remarks, or any conduct that creates a hostile work environment. It is also crucial to document positive incidents, especially when they serve to contrast negative behaviors, as this can provide a fuller picture of the workplace dynamics.

Once an incident has been identified, it is important to record it promptly. Delaying documentation can lead to lost details and diminished accuracy. When documenting, it is essential to include specific information such as the date, time, and location of the incident. Describing the context surrounding the interaction can also be beneficial. Who was involved? What was said or done? How did it affect you or others? The more detail provided, the more substantial the documentation will be. It is advisable to write down the exact words spoken when possible, as this can add weight to the documentation.

Objectivity is crucial in documentation. While emotions can run high in difficult situations, maintaining a calm and factual tone is essential. Instead of saying, "I was frustrated because my colleague constantly interrupts me," a more objective phrasing would be, "During the meeting on March 10, 2024, John interrupted me four times while I was speaking about our project update." This style of documentation minimizes emotional language and focuses on observable behavior.

Using clear and concise language is equally important. Documentation should be straightforward and easy to understand. Avoiding jargon or overly complex terms can make the information more accessible to anyone reviewing it later, whether it be HR, management, or another party involved in resolving the issue. Being concise does not mean being vague; rather, it means stripping away unnecessary embellishments while retaining the core facts of the incident.

There are various formats for documenting workplace issues, and selecting the right one can enhance the effectiveness of your records. Some individuals prefer to maintain a digital log, such as a spreadsheet or document file, where they can record incidents in real-time. Others may choose a more traditional method, such as a dedicated notebook. Regardless of the format chosen, consistency is key. Regularly updating the documentation ensures that no incidents are overlooked and that the record remains current.

It is also beneficial to categorize the documentation based on the type of behavior or incident. For example, having sections for verbal abuse, passive-aggressive remarks, or instances of harassment can create a more organized record. This can be particularly useful when it comes time to present the documentation to HR or management, as it provides a clearer overview of the issues at hand.

In addition to recording negative incidents, documenting positive interactions can serve to provide balance to the narrative. Acknowledging instances where behavior has improved or where colleagues have acted positively can help create a more rounded perspective. For instance, if a colleague who previously exhibited rude behavior has made an effort to communicate more respectfully, noting this can help to demonstrate progress and foster a more constructive dialogue.

When documenting issues, it is vital to maintain confidentiality. This means being cautious about how and where documentation is stored. Sharing personal logs with others, especially those not directly involved in the situation, can create additional complications and erode trust among colleagues. Additionally, confidentiality is important if the documentation is to be used in formal settings, as it ensures that sensitive information remains private.

If the situation escalates and it becomes necessary to report the behavior to HR or management, having well-documented evidence can provide significant support to your claims. This documentation should be presented in a professional manner, summarizing key incidents and patterns of behavior. This professional presentation can include a cover letter or statement that outlines the primary concerns, references the documented incidents, and clarifies the desired outcome.

When approaching HR or management, it is important to maintain a solution-oriented mindset. Rather than merely presenting a litany of complaints, focus on what you hope to achieve through the reporting process. Whether it is seeking mediation, formal reprimand, or simply an acknowledgment of the issue, articulating this clearly can facilitate a more productive discussion.

In the process of documenting issues, it is also vital to be prepared for potential pushback or questioning. Some individuals may deny the incidents or attempt to shift the blame. Being ready to present documented evidence in a calm and collected manner can help to reinforce the validity of your concerns. Instead of engaging in defensive arguments, refer back to the facts outlined in the documentation. This approach can help keep the conversation focused on behavior rather than becoming personal.

Moreover, self-reflection can play a critical role in the documentation process. After each incident is recorded, taking time to consider one's own feelings and responses can be enlightening. Are there patterns in your interactions? Are there certain triggers that lead to difficult encounters? Understanding these dynamics can provide insight into how to approach future situations and enhance interpersonal skills.

Additionally, seeking support from trusted colleagues can enhance the effectiveness of your documentation efforts. Discussing experiences with peers can provide additional perspectives on the behavior being documented and may even help identify instances that may have been overlooked. A supportive network can also serve as a sounding board for ideas on how to address the issues effectively.

It is important to remember that documentation is not solely for punitive purposes. It can also serve as a reflective tool to monitor personal growth and development in handling difficult situations. As one becomes more adept at documenting issues, it can lead to a greater understanding of effective communication strategies and improved emotional intelligence. This evolution can contribute to a more positive work environment and enhance professional relationships.

Documenting issues in the workplace is an essential skill that serves multiple purposes, from protecting oneself against unfair treatment to fostering a healthier workplace culture. The process involves recognizing and recording incidents, maintaining objectivity, and presenting the information in a clear and concise manner. By categorizing incidents, maintaining confidentiality, and approaching discussions with HR or management in a solution-oriented way, individuals can navigate difficult situations more effectively. Moreover, leveraging documentation for personal reflection and growth can transform a challenging experience into an opportunity for professional development. Ultimately, thorough and thoughtful documentation can empower individuals to advocate for themselves and contribute to a more respectful and constructive work environment.

SEEKING ADVICE FROM MENTORS OR HR

In the professional landscape, navigating interactions with rude individuals can be daunting, particularly when these encounters arise within a hierarchical structure where power dynamics can complicate matters. Seeking advice from mentors or Human Resources (HR) can serve as a valuable strategy in addressing these challenges. The insights gleaned from experienced individuals can provide guidance on how to manage difficult situations while maintaining professionalism and safeguarding one's career.

Mentorship plays a crucial role in professional development, offering not only wisdom and perspective but also a source of emotional support. When facing rudeness or hostility in the workplace, turning to a mentor can help clarify one's feelings and provide strategies for addressing the situation effectively. A mentor, often someone who has navigated similar challenges in their career, can offer tailored advice based on their experiences. They can provide a safe space to discuss frustrations, explore possible solutions, and offer encouragement. This support can be invaluable, as it fosters a sense of belonging and helps to mitigate feelings of isolation that may accompany challenging workplace interactions.

Moreover, mentors can help individuals identify the root causes of rudeness. Understanding why someone might be behaving inappropriately can shift the focus from personal offense to a more analytical perspective. For instance, a mentor might suggest considering external factors such as stress or personal issues that could be influencing a colleague's behavior. This understanding does not excuse rude behavior but can offer context that allows individuals to approach the situation with empathy rather than defensiveness. By viewing rudeness through a lens of curiosity and understanding, one can better formulate a response that is both respectful and assertive.

In addition to providing emotional support, mentors can assist in developing specific communication strategies. They can help individuals craft responses that are assertive yet tactful, ensuring that concerns are expressed without escalating the situation. For example, if a colleague has made a rude remark in a meeting, a mentor might advise responding with a neutral statement that acknowledges the comment while redirecting the focus to the task at hand. Such strategies not only address the rude behavior but also reinforce professional decorum. This approach can lead to a more productive dialogue and reduce the likelihood of future disrespectful interactions.

However, the role of HR in navigating workplace rudeness cannot be overstated. HR professionals are trained to handle interpersonal conflicts and workplace issues. When individuals find themselves consistently facing rudeness or hostility, it may be time to consult HR. The HR department can provide guidance on company policies regarding workplace behavior, ensuring that individuals understand their rights and the available resources for addressing such challenges.

Involving HR can also provide a level of objectivity that is sometimes difficult to achieve on a personal level. HR personnel are often skilled mediators who can facilitate conversations between parties in conflict. They can assist in finding common ground and establishing clearer communication channels, ultimately fostering a more harmonious work environment. Furthermore, HR can help individuals navigate the formal complaint process if the situation does not improve after initial interventions. Knowing the proper channels for reporting and resolving issues is essential, and HR can provide this information while ensuring that confidentiality is maintained.

When preparing to seek advice from HR or a mentor, individuals should consider the specific circumstances they are facing. Clarity in articulating the problem can lead to more effective discussions. It can be beneficial to prepare examples of the behavior in question, including specific instances that illustrate the rudeness encountered. This preparation allows for a more focused and productive conversation, as it provides concrete evidence of the issue. Mentors and HR representatives can then offer more targeted advice based on the specific dynamics at play.

It is also important to approach these conversations with an open mind. While it is easy to become entrenched in one's perspective when dealing with rude behavior, being receptive to feedback can lead to personal growth. Mentors might suggest different ways of framing conversations or modifying one's own behavior to reduce tensions. For example, if a mentor observes that an individual often responds defensively to rudeness, they may recommend adopting a more composed demeanor to prevent escalation. This willingness to adapt can lead to more positive interactions and a stronger professional presence.

In many cases, seeking advice from mentors or HR can empower individuals to take ownership of their professional journey. By addressing rudeness constructively, individuals demonstrate their commitment to maintaining a respectful workplace. This proactive approach not only enhances one's reputation but also contributes to a healthier work environment overall. The ripple effect of addressing rudeness can lead to a culture where open communication is valued, and respect is paramount.

Another key aspect of seeking advice is understanding the importance of timing and context. Approaching a mentor or HR when emotions are running high can lead to less productive discussions. Finding an appropriate time to engage in these conversations—perhaps after a particularly challenging interaction—allows for reflection and clarity. Taking a step back to process the situation before seeking advice can enable individuals to present their experiences more calmly and rationally, facilitating a more constructive dialogue.

When seeking guidance, it is also vital to establish trust with the mentor or HR representative. Building a rapport can make individuals feel more comfortable sharing sensitive information about their experiences. Trust fosters an environment where honest conversations can take place, and it encourages mentors and HR professionals to provide candid advice. Individuals should consider sharing not only the challenges they are facing but also their personal goals and aspirations. This context allows mentors and HR to tailor their guidance, ensuring it aligns with the individual's professional development.

As conversations with mentors and HR unfold, individuals should also consider setting clear objectives for the discussions. What outcomes are they hoping to achieve?

Whether it's developing strategies for addressing rudeness or seeking support for a formal complaint, having specific goals can help to guide the conversation and ensure that it remains focused. Mentors and HR representatives can provide insights and recommendations aligned with these objectives, leading to more actionable takeaways.

Importantly, seeking advice from mentors or HR should not be viewed as a sign of weakness. Instead, it is an indication of strength and maturity in a professional context. Engaging with experienced individuals who have navigated similar challenges demonstrates a commitment to personal and professional growth. It shows a willingness to seek solutions rather than remaining stuck in a cycle of negativity. This proactive mindset can ultimately position individuals as leaders within their organizations, as they model constructive behavior and a commitment to fostering respectful workplace dynamics.

Lastly, individuals should remember to follow up after seeking advice. Whether it involves implementing strategies discussed during a mentoring session or providing HR with updates on a situation, maintaining communication can reinforce the importance of the issues at hand. This follow-up can also serve as a touchpoint for ongoing support, allowing individuals to seek further guidance as needed.

Seeking advice from mentors and HR can significantly enhance an individual's ability to navigate rude behavior in the workplace. By fostering relationships with experienced individuals, one can gain insights, develop effective communication strategies, and ultimately cultivate a more respectful work environment. The process of seeking advice encourages personal reflection, growth, and empowerment, reinforcing the importance of addressing rudeness proactively and professionally. This commitment to maintaining positive interactions not only benefits the individual but also contributes to the overall health of the organization, fostering a culture where respect, collaboration, and open communication thrive.

PART IV

Maintaining Your Professionalism

CHAPTER 10

SELF-CARE AND STRESS MANAGEMENT

TECHNIQUES FOR MANAGING STRESS

In today's fast-paced world, managing stress effectively has become an essential skill, especially in environments where interpersonal interactions can be fraught with tension. The ability to navigate stress not only contributes to personal well-being but also enhances professional performance and relationships. Developing techniques for managing stress is crucial, as it empowers individuals to approach challenging situations with clarity, resilience, and confidence.

Understanding stress is the first step in effectively managing it. Stress can be defined as the body's response to perceived threats or challenges, whether they are physical, emotional, or psychological. When faced with a stressful situation, the body activates the "fight or flight" response, releasing hormones like adrenaline and cortisol. While this response can be beneficial in short bursts, prolonged exposure to stress can lead to detrimental health effects, including anxiety, depression, and physical ailments such as heart disease and digestive disorders. Recognizing the signs of stress—such as irritability, fatigue, and difficulty concentrating—can serve as a critical cue for implementing coping strategies.

One of the most effective techniques for managing stress is mindfulness. Mindfulness involves being fully present in the moment and acknowledging one's thoughts and feelings without judgment. This practice can help individuals detach from overwhelming emotions and gain perspective on challenging situations. Engaging in mindfulness exercises, such as meditation or deep-breathing techniques, can cultivate a sense of calm and clarity, allowing individuals to respond to stressors more effectively. For instance, taking a few moments to focus on one's breath before entering a difficult conversation can help ground emotions and create a space for thoughtful responses rather than reactive ones.

Incorporating regular physical activity into one's routine is another powerful strategy for stress management. Exercise has been shown to release endorphins, the body's natural mood elevators, which can enhance feelings of well-being. Activities such as walking, running, yoga, or dancing can significantly reduce stress levels. Engaging in physical activity not only helps to relieve tension but also promotes better sleep, improves cognitive function, and fosters a sense of accomplishment. Finding an enjoyable form of exercise makes it easier to incorporate into daily life, ultimately creating a healthier outlet for stress.

Developing a strong support network is vital in managing stress, particularly in a work environment. Connecting with colleagues, friends, or family members provides an opportunity to share experiences and gain different perspectives on stressful situations. Having someone to talk to can alleviate feelings of isolation and reinforce a sense of community. Support networks can also offer practical advice or insights that one might not have considered. In a workplace setting, fostering a culture of open communication can significantly contribute to stress reduction, as employees feel empowered to express their concerns and seek support from one another.

Time management skills also play a crucial role in stress management. Poor time management can lead to feelings of being overwhelmed, resulting in increased stress levels. Learning to prioritize tasks, set realistic deadlines, and break projects into manageable steps can alleviate pressure. Techniques such as the Pomodoro Technique—working in focused bursts followed by short breaks—can enhance productivity while allowing for necessary moments of rest. Additionally, delegating tasks when appropriate can help distribute the workload and prevent burnout. Recognizing that it is acceptable to ask for help can foster a collaborative environment where team members support one another in achieving shared goals.

Creating a balanced lifestyle is essential for managing stress effectively. This balance includes not only work commitments but also personal interests and self-care practices. Engaging in hobbies or activities that bring joy can serve as a powerful counterbalance to work-related stress. Whether it's reading, gardening, painting, or spending time with loved ones, dedicating time to activities that nourish the soul can enhance overall well-being. Establishing boundaries between work and personal life is equally important; setting specific work hours and unplugging from technology during personal time can prevent work from encroaching on one's mental space.

Nutrition also plays a significant role in managing stress. The foods we consume can directly impact our mood and energy levels. A diet rich in fruits, vegetables, whole grains, and lean proteins can provide the necessary nutrients to support brain function and emotional health. Conversely, excessive consumption of caffeine, sugar, and processed foods can lead to energy crashes and heightened anxiety. Practicing mindful eating—taking the time to enjoy meals and be aware of hunger cues—can promote healthier choices and enhance the overall eating experience. Planning meals ahead of time can also reduce the likelihood of resorting to unhealthy options during stressful moments.

Sleep hygiene is another critical factor in managing stress. Quality sleep is essential for physical and mental recovery, and inadequate sleep can exacerbate stress levels and impair cognitive function. Establishing a consistent sleep routine, creating a calming bedtime environment, and limiting screen time before bed can contribute to better sleep quality. Additionally, relaxation techniques such as gentle stretching or reading can signal to the body that it is time to wind down. Understanding the importance of sleep and prioritizing it as part of a self-care routine can lead to improved mood and resilience in the face of stress.

Practicing gratitude can also serve as a valuable tool in managing stress. Focusing on the positive aspects of life, even amidst challenges, can shift one's mindset and foster a sense of contentment. Keeping a gratitude journal—writing down things one is thankful for—can serve as a reminder of the good things in life, helping to counterbalance negative thoughts. This practice encourages individuals to cultivate a positive perspective, allowing them to navigate stress with a greater sense of hope and purpose.

Moreover, engaging in creative outlets can be an effective way to manage stress. Creativity—whether through art, writing, music, or other forms—provides a channel for self-expression and can serve as a therapeutic escape from daily pressures. Exploring creative pursuits can enhance emotional intelligence and promote problem-solving skills, as individuals tap into their imaginative capabilities to address challenges. Setting aside time for creative activities not only offers a break from routine but also fosters a sense of accomplishment and fulfillment.

Building resilience is a vital aspect of stress management. Resilience is the ability to bounce back from adversity and adapt to change. Cultivating resilience involves developing a growth mindset—the belief that challenges can be opportunities for learning and personal development. Embracing setbacks as part of the journey rather than insurmountable obstacles allows individuals to approach stressful situations with greater confidence and adaptability. Engaging in self-reflection and seeking lessons from difficult experiences can reinforce this mindset, contributing to long-term resilience.

Additionally, practicing assertiveness can be an effective technique for managing stress in interpersonal situations. Being able to express thoughts, feelings, and boundaries clearly and respectfully can prevent misunderstandings and reduce conflict. Assertiveness training can help individuals develop the skills needed to communicate effectively and advocate for their needs without resorting to aggression or passivity. This empowerment can lead to more positive interactions and a greater sense of control over one's environment, ultimately reducing stress.

Recognizing when to seek professional help is an important part of managing stress. If stress becomes overwhelming and begins to interfere with daily functioning, seeking support from a mental health professional can provide valuable tools and coping strategies. Therapy can offer a safe space to explore stressors, develop personalized techniques for management, and cultivate a deeper understanding of one's emotional landscape. Understanding that seeking help is a sign of strength, rather than weakness, is crucial in addressing mental health challenges effectively.

Managing stress is a multifaceted endeavor that encompasses various techniques and approaches. By integrating mindfulness, physical activity, effective time management, a balanced lifestyle, and strong support networks, individuals can navigate stress more effectively. The importance of nutrition, sleep hygiene, gratitude, creativity, resilience, assertiveness, and professional help cannot be overstated. Developing a personalized toolkit for stress management empowers individuals to approach challenging situations with clarity and confidence, ultimately fostering a healthier, more fulfilling life. Embracing these techniques not only enhances personal well-being but also contributes to a more positive work environment, where respectful communication and collaboration thrive.

BUILDING RESILIENCE

Resilience is the remarkable ability to bounce back from adversity, adapt to change, and keep moving forward despite the challenges life throws our way. It encompasses not just surviving tough situations but thriving in the aftermath. Building resilience is an essential skill in today's world, where unexpected challenges, both personal and professional, can arise at any moment. This section delves into the multifaceted nature of resilience, exploring its components, the psychological mechanisms behind it, and practical strategies for developing a resilient mindset.

At its core, resilience is rooted in a combination of personal traits, behaviors, and social supports that empower individuals to navigate difficulties. It is not merely an inherent quality; rather, it can be cultivated and strengthened over time. Research shows that resilient individuals possess a range of characteristics, including optimism, emotional regulation, flexibility, and a strong sense of purpose. These traits enable them to view setbacks as opportunities for growth and learning, rather than insurmountable obstacles.

One of the foundational elements of resilience is a positive mindset. A resilient person often maintains a hopeful perspective, believing that challenges can be overcome and that they have the skills and resources to do so. This optimism is not about denying reality or glossing over difficulties; instead, it is about recognizing the potential for positive outcomes even in adverse situations. Cultivating optimism involves actively reframing negative thoughts and focusing on possibilities rather than limitations. For example, instead of viewing a job loss as a disaster, a resilient individual might see it as an opportunity to explore new career paths or develop new skills.

Emotional regulation is another critical aspect of resilience. This refers to the ability to manage one's emotions effectively, especially during times of stress or crisis. Resilient individuals are adept at recognizing their emotional responses and finding constructive ways to cope with them. This may involve practices such as mindfulness, deep breathing, or physical exercise to reduce stress and promote emotional well-being. By learning to regulate emotions, individuals can avoid being overwhelmed by negative feelings, allowing them to think more clearly and make better decisions in challenging situations.

Flexibility is also a hallmark of resilience. Life is inherently unpredictable, and the ability to adapt to changing circumstances is vital for overcoming obstacles. Resilient individuals are open to new ideas, willing to adjust their plans, and capable of embracing uncertainty. This flexibility allows them to pivot when faced with unexpected challenges, rather than getting stuck in rigid thinking. Developing a flexible mindset can be achieved through exposure to new experiences, encouraging creativity, and fostering a willingness to step outside one's comfort zone.

A strong sense of purpose is an essential component of resilience. Individuals who have clear goals and values are better equipped to navigate challenges because they can anchor themselves to a sense of direction. When faced with adversity, a strong sense of purpose can provide motivation and a reason to persevere. Identifying personal values and setting meaningful goals helps individuals stay focused and committed, even in the face of setbacks. This sense of purpose acts as a guiding light, reminding individuals of what truly matters and inspiring them to push through difficulties.

Social support is a crucial factor in building resilience. Humans are inherently social beings, and the connections we cultivate with others can significantly impact our ability to cope with stress. A strong support network—comprising friends, family, colleagues, and mentors—can provide emotional encouragement, practical assistance, and valuable perspectives during challenging times. Resilient individuals tend to seek help when needed and are not afraid to lean on others for support. Building and maintaining meaningful relationships is a proactive way to enhance resilience, as it fosters a sense of belonging and security.

Moreover, the concept of self-efficacy plays a significant role in resilience. Self-efficacy refers to an individual's belief in their ability to accomplish tasks and overcome challenges. This belief can significantly influence how a person responds to setbacks. Those with high self-efficacy are more likely to approach challenges with confidence and determination, believing they have the skills necessary to succeed. Building self-efficacy involves setting achievable goals, celebrating small successes, and recognizing one's strengths. Engaging in activities that promote skill development can enhance self-efficacy, enabling individuals to face obstacles with greater assurance.

Another vital aspect of resilience is the ability to learn from experience. Resilient individuals view challenges as opportunities for growth, reflecting on their experiences to extract valuable lessons. This reflective practice involves analyzing past successes and failures to identify patterns and strategies that worked or didn't work. By fostering a growth mindset, individuals can cultivate a desire for continuous improvement and personal development. This mindset encourages experimentation, risk-taking, and learning from mistakes, ultimately contributing to greater resilience over time.

In addition to individual strategies, there are several practical techniques that can help enhance resilience. One effective approach is to practice gratitude. Expressing gratitude for the positive aspects of life can shift focus away from negativity and foster a more optimistic outlook. Keeping a gratitude journal—where individuals write down things they are thankful for—can serve as a powerful reminder of the good in their lives, even during tough times. This simple practice can help reframe challenges as part of a larger, meaningful journey.

Engaging in regular physical activity is another way to bolster resilience. Exercise has been shown to improve mood, reduce stress, and enhance overall well-being. Physical activity releases endorphins, which are natural mood boosters, and can provide a sense of accomplishment and empowerment. Incorporating exercise into one's routine, whether through walking, yoga, or team sports, can be an effective way to combat stress and build resilience. Moreover, the discipline required for regular exercise can translate into other areas of life, reinforcing the belief that perseverance leads to positive outcomes.

Mindfulness and meditation practices can also be instrumental in developing resilience. These techniques promote present-moment awareness and can help individuals cultivate emotional regulation and stress management skills. By learning to observe thoughts and feelings without judgment, individuals can gain perspective on their challenges and reduce the impact of negative emotions. Mindfulness practices can be as simple as deep-breathing exercises, guided meditations, or even mindful walking. Regular engagement in mindfulness can contribute to a calmer, more centered approach to life's difficulties.

Resilience can also be reinforced through storytelling. Sharing personal narratives, whether through writing, speaking, or art, allows individuals to make sense of their experiences and gain insight into their challenges. By articulating their stories, individuals can find meaning in their struggles and foster a sense of connection with others who have faced similar situations. This process of storytelling can serve as a powerful reminder of one's strength and ability to overcome adversity, reinforcing the belief that resilience is attainable.

Establishing healthy boundaries is essential for building resilience. Resilient individuals know their limits and are not afraid to assert themselves when necessary. This means learning to say no to excessive demands and recognizing when to step back from stressful situations. By setting clear boundaries, individuals can protect their mental and emotional well-being, allowing them to recharge and approach challenges with renewed energy and focus. Healthy boundaries contribute to a balanced life, making it easier to navigate difficult circumstances.

Moreover, practicing self-compassion is a vital aspect of resilience. This involves treating oneself with kindness and understanding, especially during times of failure or struggle. Self-compassion encourages individuals to acknowledge their pain without harsh judgment, fostering a sense of acceptance and self-worth. By embracing imperfection and recognizing that everyone faces challenges, individuals can cultivate resilience and a more positive relationship with themselves. This self-kindness can serve as a buffer against stress and adversity, promoting emotional well-being.

In addition to individual strategies, organizations can play a crucial role in fostering resilience among their employees. Creating a supportive workplace culture that prioritizes mental health and well-being can significantly enhance employees' resilience. This includes providing access to resources such as counseling services, stress management workshops, and professional development opportunities. Encouraging open communication and collaboration among team members can also contribute to a sense of belonging and support, ultimately enhancing resilience within the organization.

Leadership plays a vital role in shaping a resilient workforce. Leaders who model resilience and demonstrate vulnerability can inspire their teams to adopt similar attitudes. By fostering an environment where setbacks are viewed as learning opportunities rather than failures, leaders can encourage their employees to embrace challenges and develop resilience. Providing constructive feedback and recognition for effort can further reinforce this culture of resilience, empowering individuals to face difficulties with confidence.

Recognizing that resilience is an ongoing journey is essential. Building resilience is not a one-time effort; it requires continuous self-reflection, practice, and adaptation.

Life will invariably present new challenges, and the ability to respond to them effectively can evolve over time. Engaging in lifelong learning, seeking personal growth, and remaining open to change are all integral to sustaining resilience. By embracing this journey, individuals can cultivate a profound sense of strength, adaptability, and perseverance that enables them to navigate life's ups and downs with grace and confidence.

Building resilience is a multifaceted process that encompasses a range of strategies, behaviors, and mindsets. By fostering a positive outlook, developing emotional regulation, embracing flexibility, nurturing a sense of purpose, and seeking social support, individuals can enhance their capacity to cope with adversity. Engaging in practices such as gratitude, exercise, mindfulness, and storytelling further strengthens resilience, while organizations can create supportive environments that promote mental health and well-being. Ultimately, resilience is not just about surviving challenges; it is about thriving in the face of adversity and emerging stronger and more capable than before. Through dedication and intentional effort, anyone can cultivate resilience, paving the way for a more fulfilling and empowered life.

CHAPTER 11

MAINTAINING A POSITIVE ATTITUDE

CULTIVATING A POSITIVE MINDSET

Cultivating a positive mindset is a transformative process that can significantly enhance both personal well-being and professional interactions. This journey begins with the recognition that our thoughts and perceptions shape our reality. A positive mindset does not imply ignoring challenges or adopting a superficial cheerfulness; rather, it involves a conscious effort to approach life with optimism, resilience, and a solution-focused perspective. The following exploration delves deeply into the various dimensions of fostering a positive mindset, examining its psychological underpinnings, practical techniques, and the profound impact it can have on our lives.

At the core of a positive mindset lies the concept of cognitive reframing. Cognitive reframing is a psychological technique that involves changing the way we interpret and respond to situations. Instead of viewing challenges as insurmountable obstacles, individuals with a positive mindset see them as opportunities for growth and learning. This shift in perspective can be cultivated through practice and self-awareness. For instance, when faced with criticism at work, rather than internalizing it as a personal failure, a person can reframe the experience by asking, "What can I learn from this feedback?" or "How can this help me improve in the future?" Such questions empower individuals to extract valuable insights from negative experiences, fostering a growth-oriented mindset.

Developing a positive mindset also involves practicing gratitude. Gratitude is a powerful emotion that shifts our focus from what is lacking in our lives to what is abundant. Research has shown that expressing gratitude can enhance mental well-being and increase feelings of happiness. One effective method for cultivating gratitude is maintaining a gratitude journal. Each day, individuals can take a few moments to write down things they are thankful for, whether they are small moments of joy or significant achievements. This practice encourages individuals to notice the positive aspects of their lives, even during challenging times, reinforcing a positive mindset over time.

Moreover, the power of positive affirmations cannot be understated in the journey toward cultivating a positive mindset. Affirmations are positive statements that individuals repeat to themselves to challenge and counteract negative thoughts. By consciously affirming one's strengths, capabilities, and potential, individuals can reshape their self-perception and bolster their confidence. For example, someone who struggles with self-doubt might repeat affirmations such as "I am capable and deserving of success" or "I handle challenges with grace and resilience." Over time, these affirmations can rewire thought patterns and contribute to a more positive and empowering self-image.

Another crucial aspect of fostering a positive mindset is surrounding oneself with positivity. The company we keep has a profound impact on our thoughts and attitudes. Engaging with individuals who exude positivity, encouragement, and support can help reinforce our own optimistic outlook. Conversely, spending time with negative individuals can drain our energy and hinder our efforts to cultivate a positive mindset. It is essential to be intentional about the relationships we nurture, seeking connections that inspire and uplift us. Joining supportive communities, whether in-person or online, can provide a sense of belonging and encouragement on the path toward positivity.

Additionally, mindfulness practices play a significant role in cultivating a positive mindset. Mindfulness involves being fully present in the moment and observing thoughts and feelings without judgment. By practicing mindfulness, individuals can become more aware of their thought patterns and learn to identify negative self-talk. This awareness creates space for individuals to challenge these negative thoughts and replace them with more positive and constructive alternatives. Techniques such as meditation, deep breathing exercises, and mindful walking can help individuals develop mindfulness skills, leading to greater emotional regulation and a more positive outlook.

Engaging in physical activity is another vital component of cultivating a positive mindset. Regular exercise has been shown to release endorphins, which are natural mood elevators. Physical activity can also serve as a healthy outlet for stress and tension, helping individuals to feel more energized and focused. Incorporating exercise into one's daily routine, whether through walking, dancing, yoga, or sports, can significantly contribute to overall mental well-being. The sense of accomplishment that comes from setting and achieving fitness goals can further bolster self-esteem and reinforce a positive mindset.

Moreover, setting realistic and achievable goals is essential for cultivating a positive mindset. Goals provide a sense of direction and purpose, motivating individuals to strive for improvement. When setting goals, it is crucial to ensure that they are specific, measurable, achievable, relevant, and time-bound (SMART). Breaking larger goals into smaller, manageable steps can create a sense of accomplishment along the way, reinforcing a positive outlook. Celebrating progress, no matter how small, is equally important. Acknowledging achievements helps individuals maintain momentum and fosters a sense of fulfillment, further strengthening their positive mindset.

In addition to these individual strategies, engaging in acts of kindness can also promote a positive mindset. Research has shown that helping others can lead to increased feelings of happiness and fulfillment. Simple acts of kindness, whether it's offering support to a colleague, volunteering in the community, or expressing appreciation to loved ones, can create a ripple effect of positivity. By focusing on the well-being of others, individuals can shift their perspective and cultivate a sense of purpose and connection, reinforcing their own positive mindset in the process.

It is essential to recognize that cultivating a positive mindset is an ongoing journey rather than a destination. Life is filled with ups and downs, and challenges are inevitable. Embracing the concept of self-compassion is crucial during difficult times. Self-compassion involves treating oneself with kindness and understanding rather than criticism. When faced with setbacks, individuals can remind themselves that everyone experiences struggles and that it is a part of the human experience. By practicing self-compassion, individuals can foster resilience and maintain a positive mindset even in the face of adversity.

Furthermore, it is vital to challenge negative beliefs and self-doubt that may hinder the cultivation of a positive mindset. Many individuals harbor limiting beliefs that can undermine their confidence and potential. These beliefs may stem from past experiences, societal expectations, or comparisons with others. Recognizing and challenging these beliefs is essential for breaking free from their constraints. Engaging in self-reflection, seeking feedback from trusted individuals, and exploring alternative perspectives can help individuals identify and reshape limiting beliefs, paving the way for a more positive and empowering mindset.

Lastly, creating a supportive environment is key to fostering a positive mindset. This includes both physical and emotional spaces. Surrounding oneself with positive affirmations, inspiring quotes, and visual reminders of goals can create an uplifting atmosphere. Additionally, curating a digital space that prioritizes positivity—by following uplifting social media accounts, consuming inspiring content, and engaging with supportive communities—can contribute to a positive mindset. An environment that nurtures positivity reinforces the commitment to cultivating an optimistic outlook.

Cultivating a positive mindset is a powerful journey that involves intentional effort, self-awareness, and a willingness to embrace change. Through practices such as cognitive reframing, gratitude, positive affirmations, mindfulness, and physical activity, individuals can foster a mindset that enhances their overall well-being. Building supportive relationships, engaging in acts of kindness, and setting achievable goals further reinforce this positive outlook. Importantly, cultivating a positive mindset is not about denying challenges or suppressing negative emotions; it is about approaching life with resilience, hope, and a proactive attitude. As individuals commit to this journey, they can unlock a profound sense of empowerment, joy, and fulfillment, enabling them to navigate life's complexities with grace and optimism.

FOCUSING ON SOLUTIONS

In a world filled with challenges, conflicts, and misunderstandings, focusing on solutions is a vital skill that can greatly enhance both personal and professional interactions. When faced with rudeness, difficult situations, or emotional confrontations, the instinct may often be to react defensively or dwell on the negativity. However, shifting the focus towards finding solutions not only promotes a healthier emotional state but also paves the way for more constructive outcomes. Emphasizing solutions encourages collaboration, fosters resilience, and leads to a more harmonious environment.

At its core, focusing on solutions means adopting a proactive mindset. This proactive approach necessitates recognizing that while one cannot always control the behavior of others, one can control one's response. The journey begins with a conscious decision to step away from the immediate emotional reaction and instead look for ways to resolve the situation effectively. When faced with rudeness or conflict, individuals can train themselves to ask, "What can I do to improve this situation?" or "How can we move forward constructively?" This simple shift in questioning leads to a more empowered and constructive approach.

One of the most significant benefits of focusing on solutions is that it helps to de-escalate conflicts. When someone responds to rudeness with defensiveness or hostility, it often fuels a cycle of negativity. By instead responding with a solution-oriented mindset, individuals can break this cycle. For example, when confronted with a rude comment, rather than retaliating or becoming upset, a person might respond with a calm and rational statement like, "I understand that you may be feeling frustrated. How can we work together to address the issue at hand?" This type of response not only diffuses tension but also shifts the conversation towards collaboration and problem-solving.

Effective communication plays a crucial role in focusing on solutions. Clear and open communication fosters understanding and encourages all parties to express their thoughts and feelings without fear of judgment. When individuals engage in active listening, they validate the other person's perspective, creating an atmosphere conducive to resolution. Active listening involves giving full attention to the speaker, reflecting on what they say, and asking clarifying questions. By showing genuine interest in understanding the other person's viewpoint, one can create a dialogue that promotes solutions rather than dwelling on problems.

In situations where conflicts arise, it is essential to establish common ground. Identifying shared interests or goals can be a powerful way to shift the focus from differences to collaboration. For instance, in a workplace setting, employees might find themselves at odds over project direction. Instead of arguing about personal preferences, they could begin by discussing their shared objective—delivering a successful project on time. This shared goal can serve as a foundation for collaborative brainstorming, enabling the team to explore creative solutions that satisfy everyone's concerns. By emphasizing common ground, individuals can unite efforts and work toward a shared resolution.

Additionally, problem-solving requires a level of emotional intelligence. Recognizing and managing one's emotions is critical when navigating difficult interactions. Emotional intelligence involves being aware of one's feelings, understanding how they influence behavior, and empathizing with the emotions of others. By practicing emotional regulation, individuals can prevent their emotions from clouding their judgment. This self-awareness allows for clearer thinking and the ability to approach problems with a calm demeanor. For example, if a colleague is openly rude or dismissive, instead of responding with anger, an emotionally intelligent person might pause to consider the underlying reasons for that behavior—stress, personal issues, or misunderstandings—and respond with empathy.

Another crucial aspect of focusing on solutions is cultivating a growth mindset. A growth mindset is the belief that abilities and intelligence can be developed through dedication and hard work. When individuals approach problems with a growth mindset, they view challenges as opportunities for learning and development. Instead of feeling defeated by setbacks or difficulties, they ask themselves what they can learn from the situation and how they can improve. This perspective encourages creativity in problem-solving and fosters resilience, allowing individuals to bounce back from adversity with renewed strength. For example, if a project fails to meet expectations, those with a growth mindset will analyze what went wrong, learn from it, and apply those lessons to future projects, rather than dwelling on the failure itself.

Setting specific, achievable goals is also essential in solution-focused thinking. Goals provide direction and a sense of purpose, allowing individuals to concentrate their efforts on specific outcomes. When faced with a challenge, breaking down the issue into smaller, manageable components can create a clearer path forward. Each small goal achieved reinforces progress and builds momentum toward the larger objective. For instance, if a team is struggling with communication issues, setting a goal to have regular check-in meetings can facilitate open dialogue and strengthen collaboration. By focusing on these incremental steps, individuals can maintain motivation and a positive outlook, ultimately leading to more effective problem-solving.

The importance of collaboration cannot be overstated when aiming for solutions. In many situations, finding a resolution is a team effort that requires input and cooperation from multiple perspectives. By fostering a culture of collaboration, individuals create an environment where ideas can flow freely, and diverse viewpoints are valued. This collaborative spirit encourages creativity and innovation, leading to more comprehensive solutions. In a workplace scenario, for instance, brainstorming sessions that invite contributions from everyone can yield fresh insights and spark new ideas that may not have emerged in a more rigid, hierarchical environment.

As individuals engage in solution-focused thinking, it is crucial to adopt a mindset of flexibility. Rigidity can hinder progress and create barriers to finding effective solutions. Embracing flexibility means being open to new ideas, willing to adapt to changing circumstances, and recognizing that there may be multiple paths to achieving a goal. When individuals approach problems with a flexible mindset, they are more likely to identify alternative solutions that may not have been initially apparent. For example, if a team encounters an unexpected obstacle in a project, a flexible mindset allows them to pivot, explore different strategies, and ultimately find a way forward.

Furthermore, maintaining a positive attitude is instrumental in focusing on solutions. Positivity not only enhances individual well-being but also influences the atmosphere of any group or organization. When individuals approach challenges with optimism, it sets a tone that encourages others to do the same. A positive attitude fosters resilience, inspiring individuals to remain committed to finding solutions even when faced with setbacks. Celebrating small victories along the way can also boost morale and reinforce a solution-oriented approach. Recognizing progress, no matter how minor, helps maintain motivation and a sense of accomplishment.

Developing a toolbox of practical problem-solving techniques is another effective way to enhance solution-focused thinking. Various methods, such as brainstorming, mind mapping, and the 5 Whys technique, can assist individuals and teams in analyzing problems and generating solutions. Brainstorming involves generating a wide range of ideas without judgment, encouraging creativity and innovation. Mind mapping visually organizes thoughts and ideas, helping individuals see connections and relationships between different aspects of a problem. The 5 Whys technique involves asking "why" multiple times to uncover the root cause of an issue. By employing these techniques, individuals can enhance their problem-solving skills and cultivate a more systematic approach to addressing challenges.

In addition to practical techniques, self-reflection plays a vital role in fostering a solution-oriented mindset. Taking time to reflect on experiences, both positive and negative, can provide valuable insights into one's reactions, thought processes, and problem-solving approaches. Self-reflection encourages individuals to assess what worked well in previous situations and what could be improved. By understanding their patterns of thinking and behavior, individuals can make more conscious choices in future interactions and challenges.

This practice of reflection reinforces a growth-oriented mindset and fosters continuous improvement.

Ultimately, focusing on solutions is about empowering oneself and others to navigate challenges effectively. It requires a commitment to personal growth, open communication, and collaboration. By adopting a proactive mindset, individuals can transform conflicts into opportunities for connection, creativity, and understanding. The journey toward a solution-focused approach may involve setbacks and learning experiences, but with dedication and practice, it can lead to profound personal and professional growth.

Embracing a solution-focused approach is essential in today's fast-paced and often challenging world. By shifting the focus from problems to possibilities, individuals can foster healthier relationships, improve communication, and navigate conflicts more effectively. Developing skills such as active listening, emotional intelligence, and flexibility allows individuals to approach challenges with resilience and creativity. Setting achievable goals and cultivating a growth mindset provide the framework for ongoing development and progress. As individuals commit to focusing on solutions, they unlock the potential for positive change, empowerment, and success in all areas of life.

CHAPTER 12

SEEKING SUPPORT

BUILDING A SUPPORT NETWORK

Building a support network is an essential strategy for navigating the complexities of interpersonal interactions, particularly in challenging environments such as the workplace. A robust support network serves as a safety net, providing emotional resilience, practical assistance, and valuable insights when dealing with difficult individuals or stressful situations. This network can encompass colleagues, mentors, friends, family, and even professional resources, each contributing to a holistic approach to handling rudeness or conflict.

At its core, a support network is about relationships. Building and nurturing these connections requires intentionality and effort. It is essential to recognize that no one can face every challenge alone. Support networks not only offer emotional backing but also provide different perspectives and solutions that might not be evident when one is entrenched in a challenging situation. By cultivating a network of supportive individuals, one can create an environment where sharing experiences and seeking advice becomes the norm, reducing feelings of isolation and stress.

The first step in building a support network is identifying the key individuals who will form this foundation. Start by considering colleagues with whom you have established rapport or who demonstrate understanding and professionalism. These individuals can offer insights based on their experiences and may have faced similar situations. Look for colleagues known for their problem-solving abilities, positivity, or empathetic nature. Engaging with them in informal settings can help deepen these connections. Whether it's during lunch breaks, coffee breaks, or after-work gatherings, these moments can pave the way for more meaningful relationships.

Mentorship plays a pivotal role in a support network. A mentor is someone with more experience who is willing to share their knowledge, insights, and guidance. Finding a mentor within the workplace can provide a sounding board for discussing workplace dynamics, difficult conversations, and strategies for effectively handling rude behavior. A good mentor not only imparts wisdom but also advocates for their mentee, opening doors to opportunities and connections within the organization. To foster a mentoring relationship, approach someone you respect and express your desire to learn from their experiences. Be open to their feedback, and actively seek their advice on specific challenges you face.

Additionally, consider seeking support from supervisors or managers who value employee well-being and foster a healthy work environment. These individuals can be instrumental in creating a culture of respect and collaboration. When seeking their support, approach them with a clear explanation of the situation you're facing and articulate how their guidance could be beneficial. Open dialogue with supervisors not only strengthens the relationship but also demonstrates your commitment to maintaining a positive workplace.

In parallel, it's essential to connect with peers outside your immediate work environment. Friends and family can provide valuable perspectives, emotional support, and encouragement. Engaging with individuals outside of work allows for a broader understanding of interpersonal dynamics. They may offer fresh insights that can be applied to workplace situations. Additionally, these relationships often provide a sense of belonging and emotional relief, which is crucial for maintaining mental health in challenging situations.

Online communities and professional organizations can also serve as valuable resources in building a support network. Engaging in forums, social media groups, or professional associations can connect you with individuals facing similar challenges. These platforms provide opportunities to share experiences, seek advice, and gain insights from diverse perspectives. Many of these communities focus on personal and professional development, making them ideal spaces to discuss the intricacies of navigating difficult conversations or workplace rudeness.

Once you have identified potential connections, it is important to invest time in nurturing these relationships. Building a support network is not a one-time effort; it requires ongoing communication and engagement. Regular check-ins with your contacts can strengthen bonds and ensure that the support network remains active. This could be as simple as sending a message to ask how someone is doing or inviting a colleague to grab coffee. Consistent interaction fosters trust and reciprocity, making it easier to seek assistance when needed.

When interacting within your support network, practice active listening. Engaging with empathy and genuine interest helps to deepen relationships. Show appreciation for their insights and experiences, and reciprocate by offering your support in return. Building a culture of mutual support enriches the network and creates an atmosphere where individuals feel comfortable sharing their struggles and victories.

In addition to personal connections, professional development opportunities can bolster your support network. Attending workshops, seminars, or conferences related to your field can introduce you to like-minded individuals who share your interests and challenges. These events provide excellent networking opportunities, allowing you to forge new connections that can become part of your support network. Engaging in collaborative projects or group activities can also enhance these relationships, as working together fosters trust and shared experiences.

It is also crucial to recognize the role of self-awareness in building a support network. Understand your own needs and preferences regarding support. Do you seek emotional reassurance, practical advice, or simply a listening ear? Being clear about what you need allows you to approach the right individuals for support. Additionally, reflecting on your strengths and areas for growth helps you identify how you can contribute to the network. By understanding yourself, you can engage more authentically with others and create deeper connections.

Maintaining boundaries within your support network is equally important. While it's essential to share experiences and seek help, it's crucial to avoid becoming overly reliant on any single individual. A diverse network ensures that you have multiple sources of support, reducing the pressure on any one person. This diversity allows you to gain various perspectives and avoid potential burnout in any one relationship.

In navigating workplace dynamics, it is important to recognize that not every interaction will be positive. Difficult conversations may arise, and conflict may occur. During such times, your support network can be invaluable. Having trusted individuals to turn to during challenging moments can provide clarity and reassurance. They can help you process your emotions, brainstorm solutions, and reinforce your confidence in addressing conflicts. Engaging in role-play scenarios with trusted peers can also prepare you for difficult conversations, allowing you to practice responses and strategies in a safe environment.

As you build your support network, it's essential to remain open to new connections. As circumstances change and new challenges arise, new relationships can provide fresh insights and resources. Embrace the opportunity to expand your network by seeking out diverse perspectives and experiences. Engaging with individuals from different backgrounds, industries, and experiences can enrich your understanding of conflict resolution and interpersonal dynamics.

Furthermore, leveraging technology can significantly enhance your ability to build and maintain a support network. Online platforms such as LinkedIn offer opportunities to connect with professionals in your field, share experiences, and seek advice. Participating in webinars and virtual networking events allows you to broaden your reach and engage with individuals who share your interests, regardless of geographical limitations. Utilizing technology enables you to stay connected with your network, even when face-to-face interactions are not possible.

Building a support network is a critical component of effectively navigating the complexities of workplace interactions, particularly when dealing with rudeness or difficult situations. By intentionally identifying and nurturing relationships with colleagues, mentors, friends, and online communities, individuals can create a safety net of support that promotes resilience, collaboration, and personal growth. Active engagement, empathy, and self-awareness are essential in cultivating these connections, ensuring that the network remains vibrant and effective. As individuals build and maintain their support networks, they empower themselves to address challenges with confidence, seek solutions collaboratively, and foster a positive work environment. Ultimately, a strong support network is an invaluable asset that enhances personal and professional well-being, making it a vital investment for anyone navigating the complexities of interpersonal dynamics.

WHEN TO SEEK PROFESSIONAL HELP

Navigating interpersonal conflicts and managing rudeness in a professional environment can be daunting. While many situations can be resolved through personal effort, communication skills, and support from colleagues, there are times when seeking professional help becomes essential. Recognizing when to enlist the assistance of a professional can make a significant difference in managing workplace dynamics, preserving mental health, and fostering a more positive environment. Understanding the signs that indicate a need for professional intervention is crucial in maintaining personal and organizational well-being.

One of the primary indicators that it may be time to seek professional help is the presence of persistent and overwhelming stress. Stress is a natural response to challenging situations, but when it becomes chronic, it can lead to burnout, anxiety, and other mental health issues. If you find that workplace interactions are causing significant emotional distress that impacts your daily life, it is essential to address these feelings. This emotional strain may manifest as irritability, sleeplessness, difficulty concentrating, or a constant sense of dread. When stress reaches this level, it can affect not only your performance but also your overall health and relationships outside of work. In such cases, a mental health professional can provide strategies for managing stress, coping mechanisms, and techniques for restoring balance in your life.

Another sign that professional assistance may be necessary is the prevalence of anxiety or fear surrounding workplace interactions. If you experience persistent anxiety about engaging with certain colleagues or dread facing specific situations, it may be indicative of a deeper issue. This type of anxiety can hinder your ability to perform your job effectively, impact your interactions, and contribute to a toxic work environment. Speaking with a therapist or counselor can help you unpack these feelings, identify triggers, and develop effective coping strategies to navigate your workplace more comfortably.

In situations where interpersonal conflicts escalate and are unresolvable through standard communication methods, professional mediation may be warranted. This often occurs when two or more parties are entrenched in a disagreement, leading to a toxic atmosphere that hinders collaboration and productivity. When workplace conflicts remain unresolved, they can create a divisive culture, fostering resentment and diminishing morale. Professional mediators are trained to facilitate conversations between conflicting parties, helping them to understand each other's perspectives and work toward mutually agreeable solutions. If conflicts are negatively affecting team dynamics or overall performance, it is advisable to seek a mediator to provide an objective perspective and help resolve the issues at hand.

Additionally, if you notice patterns of bullying or harassment within your workplace, this is a serious matter that warrants professional intervention. Bullying can take many forms, from overt verbal attacks to subtle undermining behaviors. Such actions can significantly impact the psychological safety of individuals, leading to severe consequences, including mental health deterioration, reduced job satisfaction, and high turnover rates. If you or someone you know is experiencing bullying, it is essential to consult with human resources or seek professional guidance to ensure that these behaviors are addressed appropriately and that necessary actions are taken to foster a safe work environment.

Moreover, the emotional toll of rudeness or conflict can lead to feelings of isolation and helplessness. If you find yourself feeling alone in your struggles, unable to share your experiences with friends or family for fear of judgment, professional support can provide a safe space for expression and healing. A therapist can offer insights, validation, and strategies to help you cope with feelings of isolation while developing your communication skills. Building a supportive relationship with a mental health professional can empower you to voice your concerns more confidently, approach situations with renewed perspective, and feel less alone in your experiences.

In instances where rudeness or negativity is deeply rooted in personal issues, such as unresolved trauma or mental health challenges, seeking professional help is crucial. Personal experiences can significantly impact how we interact with others and react to stress. If past experiences are affecting your current interactions, a therapist can guide you in addressing these underlying issues. This may involve exploring past traumas, understanding behavioral patterns, and developing healthier coping mechanisms that allow you to engage more positively with colleagues.

Moreover, it is essential to be aware of the warning signs of mental health crises, which may necessitate immediate professional assistance. Signs of a mental health crisis can include severe mood swings, feelings of hopelessness, thoughts of self-harm or harm to others, or an inability to function in daily life. If you or someone you know exhibits these signs, it is imperative to seek professional help immediately. Mental health professionals can provide critical support, assess the situation, and guide you toward appropriate interventions.

When considering whether to seek professional help, it's also important to evaluate the organizational culture and resources available within your workplace. Many organizations have employee assistance programs (EAPs) that offer confidential counseling services for employees facing personal or work-related challenges. These programs can be an invaluable resource, providing access to professional support without the stigma sometimes associated with seeking help. If your workplace has an EAP, take advantage of the services offered, as they can help you address challenges while maintaining your privacy and confidentiality.

It is also beneficial to communicate with trusted colleagues or supervisors about your feelings and experiences, as they may offer insights or support. Engaging in dialogue can create a sense of community and openness, making it easier to recognize when additional help is needed.

Furthermore, fostering a culture of transparency can encourage others to seek assistance when necessary, promoting mental well-being within the workplace.

Even after seeking professional help, ongoing self-care practices play a critical role in maintaining well-being. Engaging in activities that promote relaxation, such as exercise, mindfulness, or creative pursuits, can help mitigate stress and improve overall mental health. By incorporating self-care routines into your daily life, you create a buffer against workplace challenges, allowing you to approach difficult interactions with greater resilience and clarity.

Knowing when to seek professional help is essential for navigating the complexities of workplace interactions, especially when faced with rudeness, conflict, or personal challenges. Recognizing the signs of stress, anxiety, and unresolved conflicts can empower individuals to take proactive steps toward improving their situation. Professional assistance can provide valuable tools, perspectives, and support that enable individuals to address their challenges effectively and foster a more positive work environment. By understanding the importance of professional intervention and engaging in self-care practices, individuals can navigate difficult workplace dynamics with confidence and resilience, ultimately contributing to a healthier workplace culture for themselves and their colleagues.

APPENDIX

When faced with difficult situations involving rudeness or conflict in the workplace, having a set of prepared responses can empower individuals to address challenges effectively and tactfully. Below are sample scripts tailored for various scenarios that one might encounter in a professional environment. These scripts are designed to help navigate difficult conversations while maintaining professionalism, clarity, and respect. Each script aims to provide a framework that can be personalized based on individual circumstances, workplace culture, and communication style.

1. Responding to Passive-Aggressive Remarks

Situation: A colleague makes a snide comment during a meeting about your contributions.

Script: "Thank you for your input. I understand that my approach may not align with everyone's perspective. I'm committed to working collaboratively, so if there are specific concerns about my contributions, I would appreciate your feedback so we can address them constructively."

In this response, you acknowledge the remark without escalating the tension. By inviting constructive feedback, you redirect the conversation toward a more positive and solution-oriented discussion.

2. Addressing Openly Rude Behavior

Situation: A coworker interrupts you repeatedly during a presentation, making dismissive comments.

Script: "I appreciate your enthusiasm, but I would like to finish my points before we discuss them further. I believe that this will allow us to have a more productive conversation afterward. Thank you for your understanding."

This script maintains your authority in the conversation while setting a clear boundary. It encourages respectful dialogue and allows you to complete your thoughts without interruption.

3. Dealing with Disrespectful Comments About Your Work

Situation: A colleague publicly critiques your project in a meeting, making disparaging remarks.

Script: "Thank you for your feedback. I put a lot of effort into this project, and while I welcome constructive criticism, I believe we can discuss concerns in a more respectful manner. If you have specific suggestions for improvement, I'd be eager to hear them after the meeting."

This response acknowledges the critique while asserting your desire for respectful dialogue. By inviting specific suggestions, you show that you are open to improvement without accepting disrespectful behavior.

4. Handling Inappropriate Jokes or Comments

Situation: A coworker makes a joke that is inappropriate or offensive during a casual conversation.

Script: "I'm not comfortable with that kind of humor. I think we should be mindful of how our words can affect others, and I'd prefer to keep our conversations professional and respectful."

Here, you directly address the inappropriate comment while maintaining a calm demeanor. This script sets a clear boundary about acceptable behavior without escalating the situation.

5. Responding to a Supervisor's Unfair Criticism

Situation: Your supervisor criticizes your work unfairly in front of your peers.

Script: "I appreciate your feedback, but I would like to understand more about your concerns. If there are specific areas where you believe I could improve, I would be grateful for the opportunity to discuss them further, perhaps in private. This will help me to align better with your expectations."

In this response, you validate the supervisor's role while advocating for yourself. By requesting a private discussion, you avoid embarrassment and create a space for a more constructive dialogue.

6. Navigating a Coworker's Constant Negativity

Situation: A colleague consistently expresses negative opinions about projects or team members.

Script: "I've noticed that our conversations often focus on the negatives, and while I appreciate your perspective, I believe it would be beneficial for us to also discuss potential solutions and positives. What do you think we can do to improve our situation?"

This approach reframes the conversation and encourages a more balanced dialogue. By inviting solutions, you foster a more positive atmosphere and demonstrate your commitment to collaboration.

7. Responding to a Bullying Behavior

Situation: A coworker repeatedly undermines your contributions in group settings.

Script: "I'd like to address something that's been concerning me. I've felt that my contributions are often dismissed in our discussions, and I believe it would be more productive if we could respect each other's input. I value collaboration and think we can achieve better outcomes by supporting one another."

This script addresses the issue directly while maintaining professionalism. It opens the door for a constructive conversation about respect and teamwork.

8. Dealing with Requests for Unreasonable Workloads

Situation: A manager asks you to take on additional tasks that are unmanageable.

Script: "I appreciate your trust in my abilities. However, I want to ensure that I can deliver quality work on my current responsibilities. Could we discuss prioritizing these tasks or find an alternative solution to manage the workload effectively?"

This response acknowledges the manager's request while asserting your boundaries regarding workload. It shows your commitment to quality while opening a dialogue for solutions.

9. Addressing Gossip in the Workplace

Situation: You learn that a colleague has been gossiping about you or your work.

Script: "I've heard some comments that have concerned me regarding my work and would like to clarify them. If there are specific issues, I believe it's best for us to discuss them directly rather than through gossip. Open communication helps us maintain a positive work environment."

This script addresses the issue head-on while advocating for open communication. It encourages accountability and can help prevent further gossip.

10. Confronting a Lack of Support from Leadership

Situation: You feel unsupported by your leadership during a challenging project.

Script: "I'd like to discuss the current project and the support we're receiving. There have been some challenges that I believe we could address more effectively with stronger guidance. I'd appreciate any insights you could provide on how we can navigate these obstacles together."

This response highlights your proactive approach to problem-solving and demonstrates your desire for collaboration and support from leadership.

11. Responding to Microaggressions

Situation: A colleague makes subtle remarks that imply stereotypes about your background or identity.

Script: "I want to mention that some comments made during our discussions have felt a bit dismissive of my experiences. I believe it's essential for us to be mindful of how we communicate to foster a more inclusive environment. I'm happy to share my perspective if you're open to hearing it."

This response addresses the microaggression while promoting awareness and understanding. It invites further dialogue about inclusivity without escalating the situation.

12. Handling a Colleague's Resistance to Feedback

Situation: A colleague becomes defensive when you provide constructive feedback.

Script: "I understand that receiving feedback can be challenging. My intention is to help us improve as a team, and I welcome your thoughts on how we can approach this together. Let's collaborate on finding solutions that work for both of us."

By acknowledging their defensiveness, you validate their feelings while steering the conversation back to collaboration. This approach fosters teamwork and understanding.

13. Managing Conflict During Team Projects

Situation: Disagreements arise during a team project, leading to heightened tensions.

Script: "It seems we have different viewpoints on how to proceed with this project, and that's okay. Let's take a moment to share our perspectives and see if we can find common ground. I believe that through collaboration, we can create a stronger outcome."

This script encourages a constructive discussion about differing opinions and fosters an environment where collaboration is prioritized over conflict.

14. Responding to a Lack of Accountability

Situation: A colleague repeatedly misses deadlines, affecting the team's work.

Script: "I've noticed that some deadlines have not been met, and it's impacting our overall progress. Is there something preventing you from completing your tasks? I'm here to help, and perhaps we can find a way to support each other in meeting our goals."

This approach addresses the issue directly while offering support, creating an opportunity for teamwork and shared accountability.

15. Reaffirming Professional Boundaries with Colleagues

Situation: A colleague frequently makes personal inquiries that make you uncomfortable.

Script: "I appreciate your interest in getting to know me, but I prefer to keep our conversations focused on work-related topics. I believe it helps us maintain a professional atmosphere, which I value in our interactions."

In this response, you set a clear boundary while acknowledging their interest. It allows you to maintain professionalism and personal comfort.

Conclusion

Navigating challenging workplace interactions can be complex and emotionally taxing. Having well-crafted scripts for various scenarios can empower individuals to respond effectively while maintaining professionalism and respect. These sample responses serve as a foundation, encouraging personalization to fit individual communication styles and workplace cultures. Ultimately, the goal is to foster a respectful and collaborative work environment, where open dialogue is encouraged, and everyone feels valued. The art of responding tactfully requires practice, self-awareness, and a commitment to maintaining positive relationships, even in the face of adversity. By preparing thoughtful responses, individuals can navigate difficult situations with confidence, ensuring that they assert their boundaries while contributing to a constructive workplace culture.

Made in the USA
Middletown, DE
11 December 2024